MONEY: YOUR CHILDREN, THEIR FUTURE

How you can afford everything your child needs

Sally Hamilton

SIMON & SCHUSTER
A VIACOM COMPANY

First published in Great Britain by Simon & Schuster UK Ltd, 2002
A Viacom Company

Simon & Schuster UK Ltd
Africa House
64–78 Kingsway
London
WC2B 6AH

1 3 5 7 9 10 8 6 4 2

Design: Zoocity
Typesetting: Stylize Digital Artwork
Printed and bound in Italy

Tommy's, the baby charity, is a registered charity, number 1060508

ISBN 0 74322 144 3

For Angus, Flora and Isabella

And for my mother, Helen

Contents

FOREWORD

I know the joy of parenthood. Now I know the cost of parenthood too!

As it must have done for thousands of parents before us, the financial burden associated with having children seemed ominous. So, in an attempt to understand what lay in store a little better, and with Scarlett, the first of two daughters but a few weeks old, we looked to identify a comprehensive book on children and money. Our search was to no avail.

Since launching *Jump*, in 1999 – with the specific aim of giving children, godchildren and grandchildren the very best start in life – we have been seeking to identify ways of making it easier for people, (regardless of their means) to find out where they should start when looking to save for a child's future.

Money: Your Children, Their Future is a comprehensive, no-nonsense guide. It offers parents, godparents and grandparents alike practical advice on saving for a child, short-term and long-term, and contains a plethora of handy tips on coping with the financial demands of raising children and the 'want everything now' culture.

Jump has always been associated with children, and invests in the future of young people, in all sorts of ways. We sponsor the activities of *Tommy's, the baby charity* who fund research into and provide information on the causes of miscarriage, stillbirth and premature birth. All royalties arising from sales of the book will go to this worthy cause.

Money: Your Children, Their Future fits perfectly with our values at *Jump*, so we are delighted to be associated with this unique guide.

We trust it will help steer you through some of the financial challenges that lie ahead.

James Budden
Marketing Manager, *Jump*

The savings fund for children

Introduction

As a parent or grandparent you don't need me to tell you that children cost money. Serious amounts of it. Just like us, children need to eat, buy clothes, invest in books, go on holiday and have fun. Living even an average lifestyle costs a working couple loads of money. Add in a non-earning infant and the bills shoot through the roof.

Bringing up just one child costs about £82,000 from birth to adulthood, according to recent estimates by financial group Family Assurance Friendly Society, and that excludes extras such as school and university fees. Sounds frightening, doesn't it? But if you break that figure down to the average over 18 years, it is a more manageable-sounding £87 a week.

Sensitive readers might believe the total sums are designed to deter you from taking the plunge into parenthood. In fact, these figures are meant to encourage parents to avoid money headaches in the future by getting their finances organised now. Planning ahead is a message frequently repeated by the government because it fears trouble ahead. With a rapidly shrinking welfare state, parents must now make far greater financial provision for the future, both for themselves and their children.

Financial stability

Most parents want to achieve a certain level of financial stability even before contemplating having children. I certainly did when I married in 1991. My husband and I waited for a year after our marriage before trying for a baby. We both had job changes around the time of our marriage and wanted to be sure our positions were secure and our incomes up to the challenge of supporting a new arrival.

Working mums

For me, there was no question of giving up my journalistic work after taking maternity leave. Money was only one part of my decision. In fact, if money had been the only factor, it would have been cheaper for me to stay at home and not pay for childcare. The childcare bills tore a large hole in our family budget over seven years as we juggled work with childminders, nurseries and, for a brief period, a nanny.

Hard as it seemed at the time, however, these bills were an investment for the future. I reckoned that if I continued my career as seamlessly as possible through the early years of having children, I would gain from more interesting and better-paid opportunities later on.

There was one 18-month spell when I questioned our sanity. We were spending money faster than we could earn it as we forked out huge sums both for a nanny, who looked after our second daughter when she was a small baby, and for a day nursery for our eldest because she flourished better in its sociable surroundings.

I remember clearly the pangs of envy I felt as I handed over the weekly wad of notes to our nanny, only then to watch her blow the lot on clothes and clubbing. We calculated that during that period she had more left to spend at the end of each week than we had as a full-time working couple.

Many mothers might say our course of action was madness. But we always saw the tough times as temporary and never used money as a reason not to have children. Now that our two daughters are at state school and the childcare costs are limited to their after school club we hope we are over the worst financial hurdles. You never know what might be around the corner, but with 10 years to go until our eldest hits university age, we hope we now have time to start putting money aside for our daughters' futures.

Looking ahead

As your family grows in size, so do your responsibilities.

What the birth of our children did for me was to encourage me to think about those responsibilities and view the future differently. I now look years rather than days or months ahead and inevitably worry about my daughters' future financial security. I don't think I'm unusual in wanting them to have a good start in life. It's not just about money, but money will certainly help ease their path to independence.

Most parents would like to give their offspring some kind of financial cushion when they finally flee the nest, whether it is big enough to help with a deposit on a house or pay for a car, or simply to give them the means to buy a first interview suit.

Saving plans

With our biggest costs behind us we have started saving for our children's future. I recently set up a monthly stock market savings plan for each daughter and their grandparents have given a helping hand with gifts of shares and National Savings Children's Bonus Bonds. As time goes by, and if our income permits, we will look at other options.

Getting a head start

This book aims to show you that giving your children a financial head start when they leave home need not be an impossible dream, given wise investment.

Whether you have just a small sum to put away each month for your newborn baby or a large windfall from a grandparent, there is guidance here for you.

There are explanations about the different investment options available to meet different targets. There is also advice on how to teach children about money and the best ways for them to start saving for their own future goals.

1

State help for family finance

'The story of Britain is the story of hard-working families struggling to do the best by their children.'

Chancellor Gordon Brown, budget speech, 7 March 2001

The government has repeatedly stated that the country's greatest long-term investment is in our children. To confirm that view, ministers have announced a stream of family-friendly measures over the last couple of years, ranging from improved benefits for lower income families to paternity leave for dads. Believe it or not, the state is happy to part with billions of pounds each year for British families. Even families on comfortable incomes are offered attractive incentives.

Maternity benefits

Having paid time off work when a baby is born is one of the lifelines that helps to keep a family's finances buoyant. To lose several months of pay just at a time when the spending on prams, nappies, cots and baby clothes starts to mount, can put a dampener on what should be a happy event. According to

Pregnancy magazine, equipment alone can cost up to £2,500 in the first two years.

At the moment, women are allowed 18 weeks' maternity leave and can expect to maintain all the terms and conditions of their job, except for pay – so long as they have given their employer proper notice about the impending arrival. While many employers offer more attractive terms to staff and will pay full salaries for at least some of the time pregnant staff members take off, they are not legally obliged to do so. The state tells employers that they must provide maternity benefit worth 90 per cent of salary for the first six weeks, then £75 a week for the next 12 weeks. Come April 2003, the maternity leave period will be extended to 26 weeks.

To receive maternity benefit, women must have worked with their employer for at least 26 weeks up until the fourteenth week before the baby is due and earn at least £66 a week.

A separate benefit, maternity allowance, worth up to £75 a week, may be available to those who fall through the maternity benefit net. This rises to £100 a week in April 2003.

Self-employment

I was self-employed when I was pregnant with my eldest child and so had no employer to fall back on to give me time off or maternity pay. I worked right up until the day before she was born and went back to freelancing only a few weeks later.

While I was caring for my eldest at home I received only the state maternity allowance that I recall collecting once a week from the local post office. The money was less than I had been earning, but it helped with essentials until I returned to full-time working. We were lucky that indulgent grandparents provided the baby basics, including a pram and cot, and we were showered with baby clothes and toys from all our friends.

Paternity leave

Like most new parents, my husband and I both wanted to 'bond' with our baby when she was born. With our first, he took a fortnight of his annual leave. By the time we had our second, his (new) employer generously gave him two weeks' paid leave over and above his yearly holiday allowance.

We were lucky. Some dads get only a day or two off to be with their babies. I remember my amazement at learning of the negative attitude of my brother's employer around that time, when my brother took just a single day off.

Having to rely on an indulgent or sympathetic boss will change in the not too distant future. The government has decreed that from April 2003 there will be statutory paternity leave. Working dads will have the right to two weeks' paid leave, paid at the same flat rate as statutory maternity pay. The same will apply for a parent adopting a child.

Child benefit

One crucial benefit that every family in the country is entitled to is child benefit. It is a universal benefit paid out for each child, however high a family's income.

In the tax year starting April 2002, the benefit is £15.75 a week for the eldest child and to £10.35 for each younger sibling. These payments, which are expected to rise in line with inflation in future, are made until the child is 16, or, if he or she is studying for A levels or a similar full-time course, it continues until the age of 19.

In the UK, the state offers the biggest sum for the first-born child. But in France, for example, where there are fears that the population is growing too slowly, and could leave a small number of young people paying taxes to support a large number of the elderly in the future, there are higher payments for families who expand their numbers.

Some critics argue that well-off families should not receive the benefit. But supporters believe it is important, especially where one parent is at home looking after the children and the working partner is in charge of the finances. It may be that partner will not share out the family money. If the non-working partner receives child benefit directly, then it is thought more likely it will be spent on items for the family, more often than not essentials for the kids.

Apply quickly

Whilst everyone is entitled to child benefit, its payment is not automatic. All new parents need to fill out the benefit forms soon after their children are born. It makes sense to do this quickly or else payments could be lost. The forms are available from social security offices or by phoning the Child Benefit Centre on 08701 555 540. Some mums will find an application among the free nappies and trial-size pots of baby bath in the Bounty Packs they receive in hospital.

Tax credits

Some state benefits come in the form of a reduction in your tax bill rather than cash handouts. Working families' tax credit is one of these and is aimed at helping low-income families who work and bring up children – whether they are single or two parent families. This is not a universal benefit and is available only to those families where parents work at least 16 hours a week.

The amount of savings a family has built up also affects its chances of receiving help. Anyone with savings over £3,000 will get a reduced benefit and those with £8,000 or more get nothing.

The amount of income tax reduction a family receives depends on its income and circumstances, but the average payment in the tax year 2001–2002 was around £80 a week. Parents can also receive help with childcare costs within the working families' tax credit of up to £100 a week for one child and up to £200 a week for two or more children.

Child credits worth up to around £10 a week off a family's tax are also available.

All this changes in the tax year 2003–2004 when the existing tax credits are replaced by the Child Tax and Working Tax Credits. These are state benefits rather than tax reductions and will boost the incomes of 5.75 million families on incomes up to £50,000 by £10.45 a week. Even families on incomes up to £58,000 will get some help, as will those on incomes up to £66,000 with a newborn baby because the benefits are more generous in a child's first year.

Child trust fund

Most of us only read about 'trust fund babes', the offspring of the wealthy who live off incomes from inherited investments. But Chancellor Gordon Brown has plans to give all members of the next generation their very own trust fund – whether their parents are rich or poor. His idea for these trust funds, dubbed 'baby bonds' by the media, is idealistic and is not designed to create a society of idle rich kids. Brown wants all children born from 6 April, 2003 onwards to be given a gift of up to £800 during their childhood that can be left to grow into a tidy nest egg and help give them a financial head start when they enter adult life.

The plans are still under discussion and there was no mention of them in the April 2002 budget.

Student loans

Whatever the government decides on student grants and loans in the future, it is inevitable that parents will have to take more of the financial strain of putting their children through university.

In my day – and it doesn't seem that long ago – most people I knew received some sort of grant to cover living expenses and we didn't have to worry about paying for the tuition.

Holiday work for students

It was not all easy money, however. I also did paid work during the summer vacations to help me through. Fortunately I left university not a penny in debt. Even those who did not earn during holidays did not seem to struggle too much.

In the last few years, however, student debt has become a fact of life. The maintenance grants vanished and at the moment tuition fees of up to £1,100 must be paid by all but the poorest in the 2002–2003 academic year.

For struggling students the government does offer low-cost loans through the Student Loans Company. The maximum they can borrow is £3,090 if they live at home or £3,905 if they live away. That rises to £4,815 for those who are living away and studying in London. Parents' income affects the level of loan permitted. If parents earn more than £30,000 a year their children lose out on up to a quarter of the maximum loan.

Cost of student life

Even if students are able to get the full loan, the funds are likely to fall far short of what they need to survive on. The National Union of Students calculates that student living costs well over £8,000 a year in London, including tuition fees, and £7,000 elsewhere. This means your offspring will have to either work their way through college in their spare time or during holidays or borrow from their bank – or more likely they will do both.

Customers for life

High street banks are eager to attract students through their doors because they view them as the high earning customers of the future. They will graduate with degrees and potentially get the pick of the best jobs and the best pay.

Each year, around the time youngsters have finished sitting their A-levels, the banks heavily promote student accounts. Banks also have a big presence at the Freshers' Fair, the induction event held for new arrivals at all UK universities at the beginning of each academic year. Youngsters can easily be tempted to sign up with a particular bank because of the freebies offered. They include youth oriented items such as CD players and record tokens, mobile phones and discounts on computers.

But what is becoming increasingly important to the student customer is the overdraft deal. If students haven't paid much attention to money matters before this point, then this is when they start learning. Working out the effect of interest rates that are often well into double figures, and bank charges, on their cash can give them a rude awakening to the ways of the financial world.

Useful contacts:
Department of Work and Pensions at *www.dwp.gov.uk*,
National Union of Students at *www.nusonline.co.uk*,
Student Loans Company at *www.slc.co.uk*.

2

Teaching the savings habit

'A penny saved is a penny earned.'

Proverb

There are two different schools of thought about how children turn out in life. They may end up as clones of their parents with similar characteristics and behaviour, or at the other extreme they will rebel and do everything differently.

When it comes to money, if you are a spendthrift who pays no heed to making financial plans for the future, then the chances are your children will follow a similar path. Although they might undertake a reverse rebellion and become paragons of prudence like Saffy, the long-suffering but sensible daughter of Edina Monsoon in BBC television's *Absolutely Fabulous*. Equally, parents who demonstrate too strong a love of saving rather than spending or giving money, may simply encourage their children to do as the Mary Poppins' children do and use theirs to feed the birds!

Some parents consider money a taboo subject, especially if

they were brought up in a household where it was considered bad manners to discuss it. However, what does seem certain is that the earlier you start talking about money in a balanced way early in a child's life, the better will be the results.

Ripe for learning

Research shows that children can develop good financial habits from an early age if only they are shown how.

A recent survey by the US internet company Kid Capital.com in conjunction with Dobin, a social science research group, found that children are most ripe for learning about the basics of money between the ages of seven and 13 and what they learn during this period forms deep-rooted habits for life. Between these ages, children are usually totally dependent on their parents for any money they have. This gives parents the upper hand when teaching about earning, saving, spending and giving money.

Unfortunately, the report also revealed that parents tend to wait until their children are fully-fledged teenagers before beginning proper lessons in money management. This is probably the worst possible time to start negotiating with your offspring as their changing hormones and strong desire for independence can lead to family conflict.

Prudent parents

Parents who are prudent with the family budget probably have the best hope of showing their children the true value of money and watch in relief as they follow suit. And even if you are not sensible with money, you probably do not want your children to repeat your mistakes.

The economic landscape is already different for our children and will change dramatically for their own offspring. One key difference is that they will have to make even more effort than their parents to make provision for retirement and that should be incentive enough for us to start teaching them as early as possible.

Credit card bills

In my family there is a mixture of attitudes to money. My husband is mostly cautious and avoids frivolous spending. I am afraid of being without money but have not always been great at managing it. Thanks to a combination of my husband's influence (he persuaded me to cut up an overstretched credit card in the late 1980s and not take out a new one until the bill had been fully paid off) and my 10 year career as a personal-finance journalist, I am now much more sensible with my finances than I was in my 20s.

Nowadays, I put aside as much as I can afford for a rainy day and I make strenuous efforts to avoid debt. However, like many others, I have a weakness for 'retail therapy'. Although, this involves the use of the old devil, my credit card, I now make sure I pay off the balance in full each month.

I just hope my children will follow my example. However, there are many outside influences that may lead my daughters off the straight and narrow, especially as they grow older.

Power of advertising

These days, parents have a tougher battle than ever before to resist the influence of advertising and the effects it has on children. Advertisers see pounds in their eyes – billions of them – when they think of the children's market.

Television is now crammed with adverts for toys, computer games and sweets. The supermarkets are filled with child-enticing produce such as character-branded yoghurts and drinks. Manufacturers hope children will do the hard sell for them and pester their parents until they buy the goods.

When my husband and I were youngsters, and television advertising was in its infancy, our parents quickly became aware of its potential to lead children astray. Indeed, ITV was so discouraged in my husband's family that classic programmes like *Magpie* and *Crossroads* completely passed him by.

Film merchandising

These days avoiding adverts is not as simple as banning your children from watching commercial television channels. It is impossible to screen them from the influences that go well beyond television advertising.

The 'buy me' message pervades all areas of kids' interests. Who can object to youngsters wanting to read high quality best-selling children's books? I positively encourage it. Then they are urged to go and see the film of the book. That is acceptable. But when the merchandising starts to take over and children believe that the only T-shirts to wear or sweets to eat or board games to play, are those branded with characters from the film of the book, I start to despair.

The other day I even saw kitchen towels for sale at Tesco's emblazoned with the characters from the latest children's blockbuster film.

Soccer enthusiasts receive similar attention from merchandisers. Expensive season tickets are one thing, but the regularly changing team strips and peer pressure to wear the 'right sort of trainers' all risk putting the family finances under increasing strain.

'Stealing' pocket money

The pop music market has always targeted the young. Just look at the number of bands and singers of chart-toppers who are teen idols. Ian Anderson, lead singer of the band Jethro Tull, told Rolling Stone magazine in the late 1980s something that holds true today: 'A lot of pop music is about stealing pocket money from children'.

Resisting pressure to spend

Parents can find it hard to refuse the insistent demands of children. I know from experience. One Saturday I was out with my eldest in our local shopping street that is lined with trendy gift and clothes shops and attractive toy emporiums.

Although the aim of our outing was to make a swift purchase at the florists, my daughter had a look of obsession in her eyes and attempted to drag me into almost every shop we passed. She had only £1 to spend but was hopeful I would provide any extra necessary as she eyed up bracelets, fluffy toys and books.

I finally put my foot down and the lessons in valuing money began in earnest.

I explained how I work hard to earn money for a whole

range of family essentials and luxuries and that we cannot always have everything we want as soon as we desire it. I knew I had left that first lesson a little late but I think it may be working. Now it is she who tells me off for over-spending. When I bought flowers for a friend's birthday recently, and paid a princely £35, she told me firmly and repeatedly 'that's far too much'.

Hard lessons

It can be hard for children to understand the value of money, and often it is only through bitter experience that they start to appreciate what it means.

The young son of a friend learnt a tough lesson about the value of money recently when given the treat of a fruit milkshake from an expensive coffee bar. The drink cost almost £2. He soon became acutely aware of how much things cost when he accidentally spilt the sticky liquid onto the area around the gear stick of his mum's car. It penetrated the gearbox, resulting in a repair bill of more than £900. His mother told him that was enough to buy around 450 fruit milkshakes. He was genuinely horrified.

Pocket money

Pocket money is most children's first experience of managing their own money. When I was a child it was given sporadically, usually when I remembered to ask Dad. And I tended to ask for it when I fancied spending it, generally at the local sweetie shop. Saving was not on my mind.

My husband and I decided to introduce pocket money for our children when my eldest turned six. This was set at £1 and, perhaps unfairly, has not been increased, even in line with inflation. However, she can now earn extra income by tidying her room, cleaning out her hamster's cage and carrying out other light tasks. This has started to give her some idea of what it means to earn money.

She and her sister have the bonus of looking after the large plastic bottle filled with all Mum and Dad's spare coppers, and are allowed to cash it in every six months or so and split the proceeds.

An alternative to pocket money?

Deciding whether to have pocket money at all or what level to set it is a complex issue for most parents. There are no set rules on what to do. When I carried out a straw poll of friends I found widely ranging views. Most wondered if they were doing the right thing and whether they were paying too little or too much and wanted advice on what to do.

Some wondered whether a monthly allowance might be better, with children learning to manage money by buying all their necessities ranging from clothes and books to sweets and toys. Others thought that a smaller amount that could be used to save up and spend on luxuries was more appropriate.

Pocket money strategies

Kid Capital.com's research revealed that there are three main pocket money strategies: 'conditional', 'unconditional' and 'none'.

The 'conditional' pocket money is given for household tasks so that children can understand the principle of earning. This tends to be backed up with discussions about how to save or spend the money.

The 'unconditional' pocket money is paid weekly or monthly as a means of teaching children about saving for a particular goal and prioritising their wish-list. Children are also offered the chance to earn extra cash by doing big jobs around the house.

The 'no pocket money' strategy is favoured by parents who believe that being part of the family and contributing to its well-being should not be paid for. While children in these families may earn extra money by using their initiative, they tend to be given money when they need it. One of the advantages of this philosophy is that it may encourage an entrepreneurial spirit in children.

What price?

According to a survey of six to nine year olds carried out in 2000 by financial services group Halifax, the average child in the UK earns around £1.88 a week pocket money, a rise of 56 per cent over a decade compared to 41 per cent for inflation.

Odd jobs

The survey revealed that many children top up their pocket money through earnings made from carrying out jobs around the home, with almost half of all nine year olds earning extra this way. By cleaning the car or sweeping the patio or other jobs, they can typically earn an extra £1.72 a week.

The reassuring trend emerging from the Halifax survey is that two-thirds of children save most or all of their income (around 22 per cent said they save all of it), whereas only 12 per cent spend it all.

Sweets, toys, games, books and comics are the hardy annuals of childhood spending. Although CDs and videos are coming up fast as favourite purchases, their high cost means children must first save up before achieving their goal.

Combating instant gratification

One friend, a mother of three, told me she prefers pocket money to be set at a relatively low level because saving up for something special is an important discipline to learn. Her view is that if children have too much money on tap they will go out and buy something – anything – for instant gratification. They are also likely to stop using the item within days or even hours. If, instead, they have a period of weeks to ponder the object of their desire then they can decide whether or not they really want it. The chances are the fad will have passed and their money will not be spent.

Another mum spoke of friends who matched weekly pocket money with the ages of their offspring. A few eyebrows were raised at the thought of primary school children pocketing up to £44 a month.

Positive parenting

The views of my friend with the three children are not far off those of child rearing guru, Elizabeth Hartley-Brewer. She is author of best-selling parenting books including *Positive Parenting*. Hartley-Brewer has some useful suggestions on how to handle pocket money.

She recommends giving it regularly at the agreed limit so that kids can learn about the value of money. And she suggests you get your children to list their desires over a period so that they can prioritise them. She also proposes that children are persuaded to put off their 'must-have' purchases for a week or so because they soon become less appealing. And she recommends that parents ask their kids for a contribution to the cost of a big item.

One of her tips that I have successfully implemented, after my experience with my eldest daughter, is that parents should always be clear about what a shopping trip is for before setting out. That way, it is easier to be strict once in the shops and avoid the 'purchase to avoid an embarrassing public tantrum'.

Child labour

As children grow older and become more independent, many want the chance to earn more of their own money by working outside the home. The most usual job associated with kids is the paper round.

Before you let your children embark on such part-time work, however you need to check the legal implications. There are strict laws in place, the Children (Protection at Work) Regulations 1998 and 2000, that aim to avoid children being exploited by unscrupulous employers. The main rules are they cannot take a job before they are 13 years old, they can only work a maximum of two hours on a school day (only one of which can be before the start of school) and they may only work a maximum of 12 hours a week during term time.

If your teenager is keen to take on a Saturday job, the rules are a little more flexible. If they are aged 13 or 14 they can work for five hours in total, and up to eight hours if they are 15 or over.

Most jobs for kids require a special employment permit issued by your local authority. Some jobs are banned altogether, such as working in a factory or on a building site.

Another rule to remember for working children who have jobs throughout the year is that they must take at least a two-week break from the work during school holidays.

Photogenic families

If you have a budding child actor or model on your hands, then you must seek a performance licence from the local authority. You may think a modelling or acting job unlikely. But I know of several parents whose children earn a little extra cash for photo or television shoots.

One photogenic friend and her equally photogenic young son were sitting in a local café when spotted by a talent scout. They have now appeared in several advertisements. The experience has been fun for the whole family (they subsequently all got in on the act) and also financially rewarding.

Savings habits

So how should children look after their pocket money and other earnings, however much or little they receive?

The main focus for younger children is on keeping their money safe in their own home. So a piggy bank is the obvious place to store the cash initially. Our youngest, aged six, has collected a number of pound coins from the tooth fairy in recent months, on top of her regular pocket money. At the moment the coins remain hidden in her piggy bank and she has no intention of spending her stash.

One idea for parents to consider is paying interest on piggy bank money as an incentive to keep up the savings habit.

Savings accounts

Our eldest began to change her view of money management when she reached her eighth birthday. Among her birthday gifts she received £25 in cash. She realised this was too much to store in her piggy bank. Together we also decided that it was also too much to blow on a toy, video or books.

It was now time to think about opening a bank or building society account so that she could start watching that money grow.

Beware 'free' goodies!

Researching the best deals proved to be a useful and fun exercise, especially with the internet at hand. There is a wide range of accounts available for children, most of which are savings accounts. Children do not need current accounts because they are not regularly paying bills or withdrawing money. What they really need is a straightforward savings account with the best rate of interest possible.

The good news is that children's accounts normally offer much higher interest rates than accounts for grown-ups. As with the student accounts mentioned in Chapter 1, financial institutions use children's accounts as a means of ensnaring new customers for life. They reckon that if they give kids a good rate of interest and a few free goodies at the start, then that warm feeling will stay with them into adulthood. There is little instant commercial profit to be made from children's accounts, but banks and building societies hope those children will grow up into profitable customers with a need for a mortgage, insurance and investments.

I can remember neither the rate of interest nor the trinkets I was offered when I opened a National & Provincial Building Society account as a child. Maybe neither was appealing, for I deserted the organisation long ago. That was a big mistake on my part. N&P was taken over by Abbey National in the 1990s and paid members attractive cash windfalls for the privilege!

Shopping around

For my daughter's first account we finally picked one from Nationwide, the UK's biggest building society. There were several reasons why we plumped for Nationwide. First, at that time it offered one of the best rates of interest available for children. Second, it has a branch close to where we live. Third, it is a mutual building society that pays profits to members rather than shareholders, which makes it an interesting comparison to an ordinary bank.

I'm not sure that my eldest has grasped the relevance of mutuality but if Nationwide ever converts to a bank, she will be reading a great deal about her society in the newspaper.

Another attraction of Nationwide, as far as my daughter was concerned, was the free cardboard savings box and discount vouchers that were handed out along with her shiny new passbook.

She now uses the box, in the shape of a house, to store her pocket money. When enough builds up in the box, she takes it along to her branch and has it added to her account.

Recently, she asked if she could remove some of her savings to make a purchase. My eight year old believed that to withdraw her money she would have to go into the branch and access a safe marked with her name that contained the original cash she deposited.

So there began the next two lessons about money: why she should continue to save rather than spend her savings and what physically happens to money once it is salted away in an account.

Child-friendly interest

Families should be eagle-eyed when looking for the best deals. At the time of writing, children could easily earn well over five per cent gross from the most generous organisations and on small balances, often as little as £1. But some banks and societies are less child-friendly on rates than others and if you are not careful, your child could end up earning paltry rates.

Gross interest

When children open their accounts it is important to make sure they will be paid their interest gross. Since they are (normally) non-taxpayers you need to complete the Inland Revenue form R85 that should be included with the account application form. Failure to fill it in will mean parents having to reclaim the 20 per cent savings tax that is usually deducted at source.

Taxing issues

Everyone has an annual tax allowance – even newborn babies. For the two tax years starting from April 2002 the allowance is set at £4,615. So even if your child has a paper round or does a Saturday job they would have to be earning a significant amount each week from their work and their savings before having to pay income tax.

Parents who are tempted to pile their life savings into an offspring's account to earn the best rates had better be warned.

The taxman has this loophole covered. Any money a parent puts into children's accounts will attract tax in their name on all of the income on those savings if it exceeds £100 a year (£200 between two parents).

Big business

Children's accounts are a mature business. A recent survey conducted by market research group Datamonitor on behalf of financial group Virgin Direct, revealed that kids have a total of around £17.4 billion squirreled away in savings accounts, including over £1 billion in National Savings Children's Bonus Bonds (see Chapter 3).

The survey shows there are 87 providers, most of whom offer accounts through branches. A growing number are waking up to the fact that more and more children have access to the internet at home and so are giving them access to their accounts through the net. For example, Norwich & Peterborough offers an internet account called NetmasterGold. It differs from branch-based accounts in that it is operated as a trustee account by the parent or guardian until the child is 16. The parents must have the NetmasterGold internet current account in order to open the kid's account. Children can log on to the site and learn some interesting facts about money and saving and try out a quiz about their money knowledge.

Age matters

Children under the age of seven cannot normally run a bank account in their own name. But parents can set an account up on their behalf until that age. As children grow older they can start taking on more of the responsibility for managing the account. Around the age of 11 or older many banks and societies allow them to have a cashpoint card. Children should not be able to go overdrawn on these accounts, although there have been anecdotal examples of this happening in error.

Balancing act

Brian Capon of the British Bankers' Association says: 'The age thing is not cast in stone. It's a balancing act between educating children about money and at the same time waiting until an age when they can actually sign their name and understand what is happening to their money.'

As Capon explains, the only legal restriction for youngsters involves credit laws. No child under 18 may be offered credit by a bank. He says: 'While it is illegal to offer credit it is not illegal to grant it. For example, a teenager may be able to get a £500 overdraft but only as long as someone like a parent guarantees that overdraft.'

Football accounts

For children who are keen football supporters there is a whole raft of accounts available linked to soccer teams, although the rates tend to be lower than on standard children's accounts. These deals are also available to football-mad parents. Norwich & Peterborough is one of several organisations to run such accounts, including the Canary account for Norwich City supporters. Each year the society pays one per cent of the balance to Norwich City club.

Other providers include Bristol & West, which runs an affinity account for Bristol City, Lambeth Building Society, which runs a Crystal Palace account and Manchester Building Society with an account for Manchester City.

Reaching adulthood

While the banks and societies want children to remain with them into adulthood, it does not mean they will continue to give them the best deals. To be treated as an adult in the financial world tends to mean receiving a poorer rate of interest. Most organisations switch youngsters out of children's accounts when they reach the age of 18, although a handful, including Birmingham Midshires, Britannia and Norwich & Peterborough, allow them to stay a few years longer.

3
National Savings

'Just like magic – turn pennies into pounds.'

Sally Hamilton, aged 8¼

When I was a youngster I remember National Savings, the government savings institution, working hard to encourage schoolchildren to adopt the savings habit. Many children brought in coins to buy savings stamps through the school each week. My sister has vivid memories of her savings book filled with stamps featuring the faces of Prince Charles and Princess Anne as teenagers.

When I was about eight years old I entered a competition aimed at schools and organised by National Savings to boost saving further. My fellow classmates and I were encouraged to produce a colourful poster advertising the merits of saving with the government's savings bank.

I no longer have this poster, but I clearly remember painting a large fairy dressed in pink with a golden crown and a giant wand pointing towards a mountain of coins.

My slogan was: 'Just like magic – turn pennies into pounds.' This hardly competed with the memorable advertising slogan of around that era, 'Go to work on an egg', but the judges liked it enough to pronounce me a winner.

Despite my excitement, National Savings never sent me my prize. I cannot remember what it was supposed to be but instead of learning about the value of saving, I had an early lesson in coping with disappointment.

I got off on the wrong foot with National Savings and never used it as a home for my pocket money. And in retrospect my innocent slogan was seriously misleading. There is little chance of National Savings turning a small sum of money into a mountainous fortune, unless you are lucky enough to win the £1 million jackpot on the Premium Bonds. I do own a single Premium Bond from my childhood that I received as a gift from a friend of the family, but as my continuing lack of luck with National Savings would have it, Ernie, the Premium Bond computer, has never picked that number!

Saving with national pride

There are 30 million customers who invest with National Savings (renamed National Savings and Investments in 2002), choosing it largely because its range of products, from Premium Bonds to guaranteed pensioner's income bonds, are totally safe investments. Customers like the security of knowing that the government's savings bank will never go bust. Many people also invest with National Savings as a matter of national pride, for the money it raises is used for public spending.

The price of this cast-iron safety is that the rates of return can be lower than you might find elsewhere.

Tax-efficient benefits

One big advantage of National Savings is that many of its products are tax-efficient, with interest usually paid gross. This makes life easier for non-taxpayers in particular. If you are a taxpayer and pick taxable products, you will normally have to pay any tax owed through your annual tax return. Interest rates are usually variable, although there are a few fixed rate deals.

Baby bonds

If you are saving for a child's future, then the first product you are likely to look at is a National Savings Children's Bonus Bond. This five-year savings plan can be purchased by anyone aged 16 or over for anyone who is 16 or under. You buy the bonds in units of £25 up to a maximum £1,000 for each issue of the bond. If you are taking a bond out for a godson or grandchild, you need to check with the parents that the child has not already exceeded the maximum investment. Each time interest rates change, the bond is replaced with a new issue.

The bond's interest rate is fixed for five years, at the end of which a pre-determined bonus is added. You can continue the bond after five years, but the rate earned will be the new guaranteed rate.

When general market interest rates change, whether long-term fixed rates or variable rates, National Savings will change its rates too. Rates on children's bonds normally respond to changes in long-term interest rates and are linked to what happens in the gilts market (see Chapter 8).

The bond is 'owned' by the child but until the age of 16 it must be controlled by a parent or guardian who has the right to cash it in at any time. At the age of 16, control passes to the child who can then decide whether to cash it in or leave it invested until the age of 21. The bond should not be ignored when the child reaches 21 because at that point all interest and bonuses will stop.

Tax-free

All the interest and bonuses on the children's bonds are free of income and Capital Gains Tax. As mentioned before, a parent who gives their offspring money to invest must normally pay income tax on all the interest if it comes to over £100 in any tax year, even if the child is not a taxpayer. But with these bonds, the return is totally tax-free for parents and children alike. Even if a child starts working and paying tax, there will be no tax to pay on the bond.

Birthday gifts

Some years ago I chose Children's Bonus Bonds as a regular and lasting gift for my godson, who is now almost 11 years old. When I started buying them in the mid 1990s, the fixed rates were impressive and I felt he would enjoy a decent return over time. Recently the rates have been lacklustre, so I decided to change my strategy. On his last birthday I wrote him a cheque instead. He opted to use half the money for a go-karting lesson and to put the remainder in his building society account. I liked his balanced attitude to the money and was pleased to see him enjoy some of the gift while saving the rest.

Premium Bonds

My single Premium Bond from childhood may not have come up trumps after 30-odd years but a more recent investment I made in Premium Bonds has performed a little better with the occasional £50 prize coming my way. And my youngest daughter's best friend recently received a £50 windfall despite having an investment of just £100. An excellent return, by any standard. Just to be sure I had not missed any prizes over the years, I logged on to the National Savings website (*www.nationalsavings.co.uk*). I clicked on to the Premium Bond section and tapped in my holder's number. Unfortunately, National Savings disappointed me once again. I was presented with the word 'Sorry!' in giant letters.

The chance of winning a large cash sum from Ernie has got smaller over the years. At the time of writing, the notional return on your investment was just 3.25 per cent net. That means someone with an average investment is meant to receive payouts that would work out at a 3.25 per cent net return over a year.

£1 million jackpot

The advent of the National Lottery, with multi-million pound jackpots available most weeks, forced National Savings to respond by offering a monthly £1 million prize and, as a result, they attracted an army of new investors. More than 23 million people in the UK now own Premium Bonds.

Many investors tend to view the bonds as a bit of fun. Even

if the odds of winning big prizes are against you, they still offer some of the thrill of gambling without any risk to your capital. The bad news is my £1 bond has a roughly one in 15.8 billion chance of winning the £1 million jackpot. The 'good' news is if I wanted to cash in my single £1 bond from the 1960s, I would get £1. I have lost much of the real value of the bond through inflation over the years, but at least it is worth something. You can't say that for a losing £1 lottery ticket.

The minimum purchase allowed today is £100 (maximum £20,000), although it is divided into £1 units for the draw. The chance of winning any prize (from £50 upwards) with a minimum holding is a more achievable-sounding one in 215.

Investors have to hold the bonds for a complete calendar month before they are added to the monthly draw.

Affordable risks

Premium Bonds tend to attract more attention from investors when general interest rates are low. Investors feel they can afford to take the risk because the returns they can get from alternatives are not great. When interest rates are high, savers usually prefer to see an immediate return on their investment and tend to opt for a high interest account rather than the luck of Ernie.

How to buy

Premium Bonds can be bought by anyone aged 16 or over by filling in an application form from post offices. Alternatively, you can download a form from the internet at *www.nationalsavings.co.uk*. Only parents, grandparents, great grandparents or guardians can buy them on behalf of youngsters. Bonds can also only be held in the name of one person and are not transferable.

Capital Bonds

Another National Savings option to consider for children is Capital Bonds. These are issued in different 'series' offering a guaranteed rate of return. You can invest a lump sum from £100 to a maximum of £250,000. The interest is added on each anniversary of the bond. It is best to hold the bonds for five years so that you get the full guaranteed return. You can get at your money earlier if you need to, but the interest earned will be lower, or nil, if you cash it in before the first anniversary.

If you withdraw only part of the bond, the withdrawal must be at least £100 and you must leave at least £100 invested.

Anyone from the age of seven or above can buy the Capital Bonds. Children under the age of seven can hold the bonds, but someone over the age of seven must buy them on their behalf.

The tax on the bond interest is paid gross which makes life easier for non-taxpayers. Basic and top-rate taxpayers must declare the interest to the taxman through their annual tax return.

Investment Account

National Savings also offers a deposit account for investors of all ages wanting to save on an occasional or regular basis. Investment Account savers make deposits by cash or cheque at a post office or by posting a cheque. Alternatively, if you want to make regular payments you can set up a standing order from a building society or bank account.

If you want to withdraw any of your savings you must give one month's notice or lose interest.

The account is mainly suited to non-taxpayers with the interest paid gross at the end of December each year. The minimum deposit is £20 and the maximum £100,000.

Children of any age can hold one of these accounts. The rate of interest paid is fairly unattractive considering the notice period required. You will probably find better deals elsewhere with an internet savings account or bank or building society children's account.

Ordinary Account

Some critics might say the National Savings Ordinary Account has earned its name. The account pays a lacklustre rate of interest (credited annually at the end of December) that is the same level for all balances from £10 to £10,000. It has one unique quality though that differentiates it from other bank accounts: the first £70 of interest on the account is tax-free.

Over 16s only

All the products mentioned so far are suitable for children in some way, even if they cannot get at the money until they are older. The following selection is for over-16s. So parents and grandparents with a cautious view on investing for the younger generation might like to consider them.

Savings Certificates

Savings Certificates come in two forms: fixed rate and index-linked, with a choice of two or five year terms. On both types the interest is compounded, so that you do not just get interest, but interest on your interest. Do not underestimate the appeal of compounding interest. It was once described by Albert Einstein as the greatest mathematical discovery of all time!

Fixed Rate Savings Bonds

Fixed Rate Savings Bonds let you save for a range of periods. At the time of writing the available deals were six months, one year and five years with different rates of interest paid on each. The minimum investment is £500 and interest is taxed at source. You can get at your savings before the end of the term but at the loss of 90 days' interest.

Cash ISA

National Savings also offers a cash Individual Savings Account (ISA), allowing £3,000 to be saved tax-free each tax year by anyone over 16. There is more detail on the rules surrounding cash ISAs in Chapter 4.

Stock Market

National Savings recently launched its first ever stock market-linked product. The guaranteed equity bond is a five-year account offering the maximum potential return of 65 per cent. The original investment is guaranteed. The downside is that income tax is payable on any profits.

4

Tax-free cash

'All money nowadays seems to be produced with a natural homing instinct for the Treasury.'

Prince Philip quoted in *Observer* newspaper, 1963

Cash is a popular safe haven, especially in turbulent times, when savings rates are tumbling. Even in calmer times, savings accounts are an important balance to anyone's investment portfolio, including when saving for children. They are the best home for emergency money or if you expect to need the money for your kids within the next couple of years.

The trouble with savings accounts is that the interest you earn on your money is taxed. And in periods of low interest rates that leaves savers earning even less on their hard earned money, which is why so many are attracted by anything that will pay them a return without the taxman taking his share.

One option that is particularly popular with savers attempting to maximise the returns on cash deposits is a tax-free cash Individual Savings Account (ISA). In the first two years since its launch in April 1999 to replace Tax Exempt Special Savings Accounts (TESSAs), ISAs have attracted at least £14 billion.

In April 2001, the ISA was given an extra fillip when the

rules were changed to allow anyone aged 16, rather than 18 as previously, to open one.

ISA rules

Under the current rules, savers can invest up to £3,000 a year without paying tax on the interest. And if they pick a scheme that comes with a voluntary government CAT standard that means the provider guarantees there are no regular 'charges', the money is easy to 'access' and the 'terms' are not restrictive. The interest paid must be no less than two per cent below the prevailing bank base rate and must be raised within a month of a base rate increase.

Equity investors beware

ISAs are attractive so long as investors are happy to restrict how much they want to invest in an equity-based ISA. In any tax year you may put £7,000 into a maxi plan – 100 per cent invested in equities. But you can only do this if you do not open a cash ISA in the same year. If you set up a cash ISA, then your equity allowance is immediately reduced to £3,000.

When ISAs were launched in April 1999, there were thousands of cases of investors doubling up by first taking out a cash ISA and later in the same tax year putting up to £7,000 into an equity plan. When this happens and is discovered (when National Insurance numbers are matched up) the investor is expected to close down the second ISA. For more detail on equity ISAs, see Chapter 7.

Choices

The interest rates on cash ISAs are usually variable so you cannot guarantee you will continue to get a good return on your money. A few smaller building societies offer fixed rates, but usually only to local customers who live within a certain radius of the society's branches.

At the time of writing, a decent variable ISA savings rate was around 5.5 per cent with no tax on the interest. Just as a guide, a saver wanting to earn the same net return on a standard savings account would need to find an interest rate of 6.9 per cent gross if a basic-rate taxpayer, or 9 per cent if a top-rate taxpayer. Such a rate did not exist at the time I investigated this.

It is easy to work out the notional gross rates: simply multiply the rate of interest by 100/80 if you are a basic-rate taxpayer or by 100/60 if you are a top-rate taxpayer.

Bonus interest

Always look beyond the headline rates on cash ISAs before investing. Providers often tempt customers with a high rate of interest but when you examine the small print you may find that the deal is flattered by a bonus of perhaps 0.5 per cent or 1 per cent interest that lasts for only a short period.

Chase de Vere, a firm of independent financial advisers in Bath, Somerset, that monitors savings rates, says that bonuses are fine so long as savers are aware they last a set time. It recommends that if the rate looks poor at the end of the period, or if a savings rate is cut drastically, savers should switch to another provider, so long as they are prepared to face any penalties.

Another tactic that is widely frowned upon by consumer groups and journalists, yet nevertheless continues, is when a bank or building society offers a high savings rate for a short period and then quickly shaves it back in the hope that customers do not notice and are too lazy to move accounts.

Penalty clauses

Cash ISAs were designed to be simple and easy to access. However, some of the higher-rate deals apply penalty clauses for savers who want to get at their money early. For example, you may have to give three months' notice to take out your money or, alternatively, forego the interest for that period.

TESSA-only ISAs (TOISAs)

Recently my own Tax Exempt Special Savings Account (TESSA) matured. The money I invested 10 years before that, initially in a five year TESSA with Royal Bank of Scotland and then in the follow-on TESSA with Nationwide, had grown into a useful sum. Under the old TESSA rules, you could save up to £9,000 tax-free over five years, with no access to the money unless you were prepared to lose all the tax benefits. You could then repeat the process with the original TESSA capital by opening a follow-on TESSA for a further five years.

There are thousands of people who still have TESSAs and follow-on TESSAs before they were withdrawn to new investors in April 1999.

Six month deadline

As with all savers with maturing TESSAs, I have to make up my mind what to do with the money. I have six months in which to decide whether to spend it or re-invest it tax-free.

I have no intention of spending the capital. It had already built up nicely and although I know cash will never beat a stock market investment over the long term, all sensible portfolios have a balance of cash and shares.

Like millions of other TESSA savers I had the choice either to put the maximum £9,000 in a cash ISA (or cash component of a maxi ISA) or to set up a TESSA-only ISA (TOISA). I know that if I put the money into a cash ISA, I will then limit the amount I can invest in an equity ISA for the year. Putting it into a TOISA instead, I'll be free to put my full £7,000 allowance for equities, if the opportunity arises.

Stock market linked TOISAs

At the time of writing I am considering another style of ISA plan: a stock market linked TOISA. It is still a cash ISA but the return offered on these accounts is linked to the performance of a single or several stock markets.

These accounts tend to have a fixed term of five years and either set a maximum growth level or offer a percentage of the increase of an index or indices over that period – plus most guarantee to give you back either all or most of your original investment. They tend to be offered for a limited period, so I'd better get my skates on.

Friendly society savings

Another tax-efficient and relatively safe way to invest for children is through bonds offered by several friendly societies, mutual organisations first set up more than 200 years ago. The amounts you can save are relatively small, but the bonds are popular with parents planning ahead for university fees, a daughter's wedding or their offspring's first car.

Under current rules, the most you can pay into a plan is £25 a month or £270 a year. This is in addition to your annual ISA allowance. The bonds are essentially endowment policies with a minimum term of 10 years – so you have to be prepared to tie up the money for long periods. There can be stiff penalties for cashing in early, so it is best not to start one if you think you may not be able to continue paying into the plan. The penalties are most onerous in the early years.

University costs

Parents or grandparents who are saving for children tend to set up a plan to mature further in the future, perhaps when they reach a key age such as 18, when they may want to go to university, for example.

For tax purposes, these policies have to offer a small amount of life insurance, which comes into effect only when the child reaches the age of 10. A child is only allowed to hold one bond.

Because the returns are tax-free they are most attractive to top-rate taxpayers.

Varied funds

The friendly society invests your money in a fund whose managers buy a wide range of investments including shares, fixed interest securities and property. The two main types of funds are unit-linked and with-profit. Unit-linked funds operate like a Unit Trust and can rise and fall in value each year, depending on the state of the sectors they are invested in.

With-profits funds add a bonus to your investment each year using a process called 'smoothing' (more of that in Chapter 6), with some money held back in good years by the fund managers so that bonuses can also be paid out in the bad. This is meant to even out the ups and downs of investment performance over the years.

The annual bonus cannot be taken away once it is announced. There should also be a terminal bonus when the plan matures, but there is no way of knowing how large or small that will be.

High charges

One criticism levelled at these plans is the relatively high management charges. Friendly societies' defence is that it is comparatively expensive to manage large numbers of low value accounts. They would like to accept larger contributions, which would make their operations more economical, but legislation prevents them.

Accurate information about performance can be hard to come by. Make sure you ask your chosen friendly society for performance data before signing up so that you can compare it with other investment options.

Not all friendly societies offer children's bonds. Check with the Association of Friendly Societies by phoning 020 7397 9550 or writing to 10–13 Lovat Lane, London EC3R 8DT.

5 Stocks and shares

'You need to speculate to accumulate.'

Old stock market adage

Parents who tuck away cash in a bank or building society account or with National Savings can build up reasonable sums for themselves or their children over time. These products play a crucial role in any investment strategy, especially if you have a short period of one or two years in which to save for your goal.

Investors with National Savings or a bank or building society can relax in the knowledge that the organisation holding their money is unlikely to go bust. Even if a bank or building society were to go under, there are schemes to protect the lion's share of your money.

Depositor protection

Both banks and building societies are members of the Financial Services Compensation Scheme introduced in December 2001.

The scheme covers the first £2000 in full of your savings and 90 per cent of the next £33,000 (so a maximum of £31,700) if the worst happens. Nervous investors with cash savings in excess of the maximum payout can think about spreading the money between different institutions.

The main problem with piling cash into a deposit account is not that you are going to lose it, but that whatever level of interest it earns, it will sit there at the mercy of inflation. Even in these low inflation times the real value of your hard-earned savings will be eaten away over time.

In order to accumulate real wealth, parents need to be prepared to take more risk with at least some of their money and put a proportion into equities, otherwise known as **stocks and shares**.

Wealth warning

Equities are the place to make money, although there are no guarantees. Independent financial advisers warn that you should only take the plunge into the stock market if you are certain you understand the risks and are prepared to live with them. There is always a chance you could lose your shirt if a company collapses or there is a stock market crash, so you should never invest if fears over any potential losses leave you tossing and turning in bed at night. Nor should you consider buying shares if any losses from the investment would have a damaging effect on your lifestyle.

Remember that when calculating the potential loss from an investment, it is not only the capital that you will lose but also any income it generated.

Beat the building society

If you feel you are in a position to invest without losing sleep, then you should also be prepared to take the long view. If you can leave that money untouched for a long period, then you are likely to be rewarded with returns that outpace those of a building society.

The argument is that stock markets may lurch upwards and

downwards over the period you invest, but that, if you sit tight, the end result should prove more favourable than leaving the money on deposit. All the historical evidence points to this trend, although history will not necessarily repeat itself.

Shares versus cash

There is plenty of evidence to suggest your share investment will perform pleasingly. The influential Barclays Capital Equity-Gilt Study, which compares the performance of different categories of investment over time, illustrates how shares manage to outperform cash over long periods. The 2001 edition shows that over the 10 years to the end of 2000, the annual real return from equities was 11.8 per cent compared with 4.2 per cent from cash and 9.4 per cent from gilts (see Chapter 6). Over 20 years the annual figures were 11.8 per cent, 4.7 per cent and 7.7 per cent respectively. Look back over a century and the evidence remains persuasive. Equities returned 5.5 per cent each year, cash 0.9 per cent and gilts 1.1 per cent.

The short-term picture reveals just why equity investors need a steady nerve through turbulent times. According to Barclays Capital, during the year 2000, the year when investors piled in to technology shares only to see the sector suddenly collapse, returns on equities fell by 8.6 per cent, while cash rose 3.2 per cent and gilts 6.1 per cent.

Reinvesting dividends

An important issue to think about when investing in equities is what to do with the dividends. If you don't need them for income which you probably won't if you're saving for your children, then it makes sense to reinvest them as it helps to compound the value of your portfolio. Had £100 been invested on the stock market in 1899, but the income taken during the following 101 years, the value of the shares would have grown to just £233 in today's terms. However, if all the income had been reinvested, the value would have risen to a tidy £22,817, according to the Barclays Capital survey.

Single shares

Even if you are convinced that the stock market should be a home for at least some of your money, how do you decide what to invest in? One golden rule about investing is not to put all your eggs in one basket. It's a wise motto. To invest all your money in a single share is asking for trouble. If that company goes bust, you may lose everything.

If you spread your money across half a dozen shares or more in different market sectors you can reduce your overall risk. You can then afford for a couple of your chosen shares to do badly and hope the others make up for their poor performance.

Attitude to risk

With the diversification rule in mind, it is then up to you to decide on which types of shares to buy. The choice will depend on a range of factors including the strength of your own financial position, what you feel about risk and your knowledge of the different sectors.

Income or growth?

The type of share you pick also depends on whether you are aiming to create income or growth from your investment, or a mixture of the two; also, on whether you are a beginner or a seasoned investor with a wide range of shares and share buying experience under your belt.

Since it is your child's future you are saving for, then it is likely that you will be considering shares that offer the best growth potential over five, 10 or 15 years. The options range from buying a solid blue chip name to a little known new arrival on the UK market or even a share on an overseas stock market.

Just as someone looking for an income cannot guarantee their chosen share will continue to pay high dividends, so someone picking a share for its growth potential cannot be sure it will live up to expectations. Millions of investors thought that buying a technology share in early 2000 would lead to guaranteed growth. Not long afterwards, the technology sector bombed, leaving the same shareholders nursing significant real or paper losses.

Rocky patch

Even sticking with a blue chip share can have its rocky moments. You could not get more blue chip than my first exposure to a stock market investment. When my Granny died in the early 1980s, she left me a few hundred Marks & Spencer shares, which I still own. It's no secret that Marks & Spencer went through a sticky patch, particularly in 2000, when the value of the shares dropped sharply. I held on to the shares through thick and thin because I believe there is no point in selling low, especially when in this case I didn't pay for the shares in the first place. I also had a sentimental attachment to the shares, and I figured that I had earned reasonable dividends over the years and would have probably fared worse with a building society.

At the time of writing my decision to sit tight looks like paying off as M&S was the best performing FTSE 100 share of 2001. But who knows what will happen in the future?

Confusing language

Many small investors are nervous about taking their first steps into the stock market. The City can seem daunting, with many viewing it as a pin-striped old boys' club full of fusty old stockbrokers speaking their own secret language. But private investing in the UK has undergone a revolution that has helped sweep away the old image and create a new style of stockbroker.

Investor revolution

The big changes first began with the introduction, in 1979, of the first employee shares schemes. Then came the privatisation of a string of national companies, including British Telecom and British Gas during the Thatcher era of the 1980s, which created an army of private investors, dubbed 'Sids'.

In a short space of time a whole new breed of investor grew up demanding a different type of service.

The revolution continued throughout the 1990s as millions of savers and borrowers with building societies became shareholders as a result of demutualisation. When building societies such as Abbey National, Halifax and Alliance & Leicester decided to convert into banks and float on the stock market, members were offered share and cash windfalls totalling billions of pounds as compensation.

Educating shareholders

In the early days of demutualisation there was some confusion among the newly created shareholders about what conversion from a bank to a building society really meant. Some former members did not understand that they now owned a share in the converted company. Nor did they understand why they earned an income through twice yearly dividends.

When Abbey National, the first building society to float on the stock market, issued its first dividends to shareholders, many debut shareholders thought the dividend voucher was a demand for money rather than a payment to them! As the demutualisation bandwagon rolled on, however, shareholders became more knowledgeable and sophisticated and began to understand how shareholdings worked.

The converting societies also helped; they tried harder to get the message across about the effects of demutualisation, publishing more detailed booklets and factsheets about the implications of being a shareholder.

Retirement provision

Another influence on the demystification process is the declining welfare state. Concerned about how to pay for retirement, more people have turned to shares in a bid to build an adequate pot of money to help them through their twilight years.

All these influences have helped to create around 12.5 million private shareholders, more than four times the number in 1979, according to ProShare, the organisation that promotes wider share ownership.

Building a portfolio

If you intend to build up your own portfolio of individual shares you need to be prepared to devote plenty of time to acquiring the right knowledge and expertise. This includes scouring the financial sections of newspapers and the specialist press for information on individual companies. The internet is another useful tool for serious investor research.

It is important to keep a close eye on the trends in share price performance and other important factors affecting your investment.

There are some important terms and issues to think about when considering buying shares.

Total return

I've already mentioned that individual shares offer the potential for two types of return: an income from the dividend, normally paid twice yearly, and capital growth. You will come across the term 'total return' which is the two put together.

The amount of dividend you receive will vary each time but most companies like to raise it, or at least maintain it, if possible. If a company is a relative newcomer to the market and needs to re-invest every penny in the business, or if it is experiencing hard times, it may reduce the dividend or miss it altogether.

Your dividends are taxed at source and this tax cannot be reclaimed. If you are a higher rate taxpayer you must pay extra tax on the income through your annual tax return.

Capital gains

As a shareholder you will also hope to make a capital gain on your investment. But that will depend on what price you buy and sell at. And remember that you do not crystallise any gain (or loss) until you sell.

Selling at a loss is not necessarily a bad thing. It can be sensible tax-planning. It may be possible to offset losses against any gains from the sale of other investments in a tax year.

If you play your cards right your annual capital gains may stay within your annual exemption of £7,700 in the tax year 2002–2003. The tax rules are complicated, so it makes sense to consult an accountant or independent financial adviser before making any rash moves.

Transferring shares

Another sensible tax-saving initiative for married couples is to think about transferring shares into the name of one or other partner. This can be useful for two reasons. First, if one partner is on a lower tax rate than the other then the dividends will attract less tax. Second, you each have your own annual Capital Gains Tax exemption.

There is another way to avoid tax on your shares. You can shelter up to £7,000 a year from both income and Capital Gains Tax in a self-select maxi Individual Savings Account. For more detail on tax-free stock market ISAs, see Chapter 7.

Keeping tabs

Watching the price performance of your share is just one of the ways of keeping tabs on your investment – although you should not read too much into daily ups and downs. The longer-term trend is more important and how its performance compares with that of other companies in its sector.

Also, it is important not to look at your portfolio in isolation. If over a year it falls in value by five per cent that needn't be as bad as you think. If the market overall has fallen 10 per cent, then you have done relatively well. But if your investment rises by only five per cent in a market that has risen by 10 per cent, then you have done relatively badly.

Keen investors should also be prepared to scrutinise any annual reports they receive as they are a mine of useful information that can help you decide if your investment is on track.

Essential jargon

There is also essential jargon to learn. Once learnt, it can give you the confidence to make informed decisions about the shares you hold in your portfolio.

Here is an explanation of some of the main terms:

Price/earnings ratio: This ratio helps an investor work out how confident the market feels about a particular share. You can find it published alongside the share price in the daily papers. The ratio is worked out by dividing the share price by the earnings per share. A high ratio normally means the shares are in demand because high growth is anticipated. The average for the FTSE 100 (top 100 UK listed companies) and FTSE All Share (top 800 companies) was around 18 at the time of writing. Compare that to the software and computer services sector with its ratio of around 40 at that period.

Earnings per share: This is the amount of profit assigned to each ordinary share. It is worked out by dividing profits after tax and extraordinary items by the total number of ordinary shares. It is important to monitor trends in earnings per share and compare with shares in the same sector. Ideally, earnings should show steady growth.

Return on capital employed: This reveals how well the management of your chosen company is using the capital available to generate profits. You work it out by dividing profits before tax and interest on loans by capital employed and then express as a percentage. A decent return would be around 20 per cent, which means every £100 of capital produces £20 of profit.

Dividend yield: This is the dividend payment on your shares expressed as a percentage of the share price. It is calculated by dividing the dividend per share by the share price and then by multiplying the result by 100. The average for FTSE 100 and FTSE All Share companies in October 2001 was just under three per cent.

Dividend cover: This figure shows you how many times a company can pay the annual dividend from earnings. It is calculated by dividing earnings per share by the dividend. Dividend cover of more than one suggests that the company is retaining profits, hopefully to invest for growth. Less than one suggests the company may be drawing on its reserves.

Buying shares

You normally have to buy and sell shares through a stockbroker. What you pay will depend on the type of service you need.

Whatever option you pick, there are standard charges to pay, including 0.5 per cent stamp duty (minimum £5 a trade) that goes to the government, and on trades of £10,000 or above there is a small levy that goes to help towards the cost of running the Panel on Takeovers and Mergers.

There is no minimum investment for individual shares. But considering the dealing charges involved, it makes sense to make a minimum investment of £1,000 to £2,000 – and remember, you will be charged again when you sell them (although not stamp duty, as it is only charged on purchases).

When you ask your broker for a price on a particular share, you will be quoted both the 'sell' (also known as 'bid') price, the price at which you can sell your shares, and the 'buy' (also known as 'offer') price, the price at which you can buy the shares. The sell price is lower than the buy price and the difference between the two is called the 'spread'.

Broker services

There are three types of service to choose from: execution-only, discretionary and advisory.

Execution-only

Another factor that has helped give small investors easier access to the stock market is the growth in supply of execution-only stock broking. This means investors can buy and sell without seeking any advice first.

Shareholders who know what they want to trade in can do it quickly and cheaply over the phone or through the internet. The advent of internet trading in particular helped boost shareholder numbers by 500,000 in 1999 alone, according to ProShare estimates.

Execution-only buying and selling is the cheapest way to trade. But the commission rates and dealing charges do vary from broker to broker, so it is essential to shop around.

When you have chosen a broker you will have to set up an account and in some cases may also have to deposit some cash in the account before you start trading.

Discretionary broker

If you have neither the time nor the inclination to spend researching the market and particular shares, you can hand over the entire job to a discretionary broker. If you take this route, the broker will make all the buying and selling decisions at its 'discretion'.

Because it is a full service it will cost you more in charges. The broker will try and make its decisions based on your overall aims. You should give some idea of your goals when you set up the arrangement. For example, if you want capital growth from your investment, the broker will know to choose shares likely to increase in value. If you want income, on the other hand, then the broker will know to stick with shares that are likely to produce rising dividends.

Advisory broker

If you want advice on which shares to buy and sell then you can appoint an advisory broker. The broker will do the trading for you, but should check with you in advance that you are happy with the advice. When you set up the arrangement you will normally be asked to describe your investment goals. As well as paying dealing commission you may also have to pay an annual management fee based on the value of your investments.

If you want to find a broker, contact the Association of Private Client Investment Managers and Stockbrokers at 112 Middlesex Street, London E1 or visit *www.apcims.co.uk*.

Certificates or nominee?

The traditional way to hold a share is in the form of a share certificate. When you buy a share, the certificate is posted to you. You must keep it somewhere safe, either at home or with your bank, because when you decide to sell your shares you need to send the certificate to your broker.

Because this is a bureaucratic, time-consuming and expensive way to manage shares, there is a growing trend towards a paperless system, and the settlement of share trades can now be carried out quickly through an electronic system called Crest.

In order for shares to be settled through Crest, they have to be held in so-called 'nominee' accounts with a bank or broker, and to be registered in the name of the nominee account.

The legal ownership of the shares belongs to the nominee company but you hold on to the 'beneficial interest'. That means any growth in the value or any income from the shares is yours. You need to ask the nominee company a range of questions before going ahead, such as what charges are there for holding your shares, when do you get your dividends and how is your investment protected.

Ordinary shareholders have a range of rights, including voting on any important decisions being made by the company.

If you hold your own certificates you will automatically receive annual reports and any perks, such as discounts off the product or service offered by the company whose shares you own. These are not automatically available if you hold your shares in a nominee account. However, you can ask your broker to make sure you get them.

In whose name?

Although minors can hold shares, no one under the age of 18 can normally buy and sell them. This is simply because few stockbrokers are likely to want to take on the risk.

Diane Hay, chief executive of ProShare, says: 'Few people want to deal with children directly because the law says you cannot sue a minor. So if a youngster were to call a broker up to buy 10,000 shares but failed to come up with the money to pay for them, there would be nothing the broker could do about it. It cannot come after the parents for that money.'

But that does not mean children do not own shares in their own name. Hay says: 'Many children inherit shares. And there are companies who pay staff bonuses in shares. I know of several 16 year olds who have received a few shares from their regular Saturday job with Sainsbury's, for example.'

Bare trusts

Realistically, the best way to invest in shares for your offspring is to buy them yourself and then designate them in the child's name.

You will still be the legal holder and will make any decisions regarding the investment.

A sensible approach is to create a bare trust for the shares. This is a simple legal document that allows you to hold the shares on behalf of your child. The income and the capital must be left to accumulate until your child reaches at least 18. However, if the income exceeds £100 in any tax year, then all the income will be treated as part of your own income for tax purposes. For that reason, it can make sense to choose shares that are more likely to produce a capital gain when they are eventually sold, rather than income.

A child has the same annual Capital Gains Tax exemption as an adult, which can be used if the shares are sold.

Generous grandparents

If a grandparent takes out shares in the name of a grandchild, and puts the shares in to a bare trust, then the rules are different. Any income from the investment is taxed as the child's rather than the grandparent's. Since everyone, including a newborn baby, has a personal tax allowance (£4,615 for the tax year 2002–2003), it is unlikely the child would face an income tax bill. The same Capital Gains Tax rules apply as before. However, there could be inheritance tax implications for grandparents. For further details see Chapter 13.

Investor protection

As with building society and bank savings, investors dealing through a broker are offered protection against the company going out of business and taking their money with them. The Financial Services Compensation Scheme pays the first £30,000 of a valid claim in full and 90 per cent of the next £20,000. That means the maximum payout is £48,000.

Further reading: ProShare has a useful guide to the ins and outs of investing called *The Investor's Handbook*. Visit *www.proshare.org* for more details.

6 Collective investments

'By uniting we stand, by dividing we fall.'
From, The Liberty Song, John Dickinson 1768

Direct investment in the stock market can be an expensive and risky option for many investors. Most financial experts suggest you need a minimum of £10,000 to create a sensible portfolio of a dozen or so single shares. Less than that and the costs and risks are too high.

However, investing in the stock market is not just about picking individual shares and spending serious amounts of money. There are many ways of getting exposure to equities for relatively small investments and at a reduced level of risk. At the same time it is possible to remove the need for investors to make constant decisions about which shares to buy and sell, which can be ideal for adults saving on behalf of children.

Unit Trusts, Open Ended Investment Companies (OEICs) and Investment Trusts are three popular routes into the stock market that can spread the risk and limit costs for small investors. The three types are structured differently, but what they have in common is that they are collective funds that pool the money of a large number of small investors into a single pot that is then used to buy dozens or sometimes hundreds of shares or other types of investment. With such a broad exposure to different shares, the idea is that an investor's initial capital should not be badly hit if one or two of the underlying investments do badly.

Instead of individuals making the decisions about which shares to pick, professional managers take control of the funds and use their expertise to select shares and decide the best time to buy and sell.

Rise and fall

Just because collective funds aim to spread the risk, it does not mean they are risk free. The value of your investment can rise and fall, just as shares prices do, especially if there is a general market upheaval. With that in mind, savers should only invest in funds if they are prepared to stick with them for the medium to long term – which means at least five to ten years. By holding on patiently, your investment is likely to produce a return that will outpace building society returns and give your children a better head start in life.

Just as buying a single share has its risks, investing in a single fund can be a gamble too. Therefore it can be sensible to spread risk further by investing in more than one fund or type of fund.

Start small

The big attraction of Unit Trusts, OEICs and Investment Trusts is that investors can start saving for their children with as little as £25 to £50 a month or make lump sum investments from between £500 and £1,000.

Unit Trusts

When you invest in a Unit Trust you become a 'unit holder' of the fund. You do not own the shares in the underlying fund. A Unit Trust is also an 'open-ended' fund. That means the size of the fund fluctuates when investors buy and sell their units.

OEICs are a more modern version of a Unit Trust with a

different structure and way of charging, but they have similar goals. Both an OEIC and a Unit Trust can have holdings in any number of companies but the regulations mean neither type can put more than 10 per cent of the total fund into any one company.

Unit Trust and OEIC prices relate directly to the value of the fund's underlying assets and are published in leading daily and weekly newspapers and magazines and specialist monthly publications such as *Money Management*, *Bloomberg Money*, *Financial Mail Money* and *Money Observer*.

Pricing

Unit Trusts have two prices, the 'offer' price, the one that you buy at, and the 'bid' price, that you sell at. The 'spread' between them is usually at least five per cent and normally includes the initial charge that you pay for setting up your investment. Your investment needs to rise by the amount of the spread before you make any money.

Both types of funds carry annual management charges ranging from 0.5 to 1.5 per cent of your investment. Riskier funds that need more hands-on management tend to attract higher annual charges.

Investment Trusts

An Investment Trust differs from a Unit Trust in that it is set up as a company that is quoted on the stock market. The company's business is to invest in the shares of other companies.

Unlike a Unit Trust or OEIC, an Investment Trust is a closed-ended fund. This means the amount invested in the fund is set at the time of launch and a fixed number of shares is issued. Because the initial fund is a finite size, the price of the shares will fluctuate depending on demand and will not directly relate to the value of the fund's assets. This tends to make Investment Trusts more volatile than Unit Trusts.

Discounts and premiums

When you look up the prices of Investment Trust shares in a newspaper you will see a column that shows whether they are trading at a 'discount' or at a 'premium'. If at a discount that means the share price is less than the value of the underlying assets; at a premium means the price is higher than the value of the underlying investments.

If you buy at a premium then you are paying more for the whole than the sum of the parts. In other words, you may not be getting value for money. Conversely, if you buy at a discount then you are getting more than the sum of the parts. This can mean you have bought at a bargain price. But that is of little consequence if the shares never move from trading at a discount.

Gearing

Unlike Unit Trusts, Investment Trusts are allowed to borrow money against their assets in order to make further investments. This is known as 'gearing' and in a rising market can help fund managers achieve better returns because the Investment Trust has got greater exposure to the market. However, a falling market can lead to bigger losses, especially for highly geared trusts. The role of the Investment Trust fund managers is to react to such changing conditions and in a falling market they will normally reduce gearing.

Investors usually buy and sell Investment Trust shares through a stockbroker or by investing through an Investment Trust savings plan (see below).

The splits

You may have read some of the widespread comment about split-capital Investment Trusts in recent months. These are a relatively recent addition to the Investment Trust family and are funds divided into two or three different classes of shares to meet different investment goals. They offer income shares for those who only want income from their investment, capital shares for those who are focusing only on growth and a third option called zero dividend preference shares, called zeros for short, that offer a set amount of growth agreed at the outset but no income. Parents often use zeros as part of school fees planning (see Chapter 10 for more details on how to use them).

Which fund?

Just as you have to make decisions about your savings goals when buying individual shares, you also have to think about what you want from a collective investment. Do you want capital growth or income, or a mixture of the two? Are you ultra-cautious or do you want to take more risk with your money? How long have you got until you need to cash in the investment?

And as high-risk shares offer the potential of high rewards or losses, so too do the high-risk funds. If you cannot afford to take big risks with your money or are a first-time investor, then it usually makes sense to select a more cautious fund such as one that invests in well-known UK companies.

High-risk

If you are a more experienced investor, or already have plenty of UK market exposure, you can add some spice to your portfolio with a high-risk fund such as technology or emerging markets. But as with high-risk shares, you need to be sure you can live with the consequences of losing all of your investment.

The choice is not just between high-octane versus ultra-cautious investments. There are innumerable options in between, from the outer limits of specialist funds and single country funds such as those investing only in Japan to the safer havens of cash funds that are similar to deposit accounts and funds that specialise in corporate bonds (see Chapter 8).

If you have no idea what is available, a good starting point is to get a full list of Unit Trusts and OEICs from the Investment Management Association (IMA) by phoning 020 7831 0898 or visit IMA's website at *www.investmentuk.org*. For information on Investment Trusts, contact the Association of Investment Trust Companies (AITC) by phoning 020 7282 5555 or visit *www.aitc.co.uk*.

Index trackers

Most collective funds employ managers to make the investment decisions. Their main aim is to beat the market in their chosen investment area. They are called active funds.

There is another type of fund that is managed on a 'passive' basis. These are called index-tracker funds and are set up to mirror the performance of a particular stock market index, such as the FTSE 100 or the FTSE All Share or even an international index. They can be an attractive investment in a rising market, but because they track an index, they will also mirror its performance when it falls.

Because index funds are not actively managed, the charges are usually much lower than for active funds. Critics suggest that in the long term, active management will produce better returns, despite the higher costs. Index-tracker supporters beg to differ.

Ethical investing

A growing trend in the modern world is towards ethical investment and this may be an area worth considering if you are making an investment for the next generation. Young people often take an even greater interest in ethical and environmental issues than their parents or grandparents, with many youngsters being taught the importance of the ecological three 'r's, re-use, recycle and reduce waste, at school.

My daughters' school is active in educating the pupils in this area and my eldest in particular is aware of the threat to the environment that pollution and waste present. Older children may also have strong views on wider issues such as animal testing or exploitation of third world countries and the destruction of the rain forest. Or your child or grandchild might simply be vegetarian.

If your children or grandchildren are interested in environmental and social issues, they may like that to be reflected in any investment you make on their behalf, therefore.

Fast growing sector

It is becoming easier to invest according to your principles with a rapidly increasing number of ethical funds to choose from. Although ethical investment represents just two per cent of the investment fund market, it is worth around £4 billion and is one of the fastest growing sectors with around 60 funds to choose from.

FTSE International saw enough potential in the future of this sector to launch a series of FTSE4Good indices devoted to monitoring the performance of ethical shares with indices covering UK, European and global firms.

Where it started

Early ethical investment (the first fund was launched in 1984) was based around funds that refused to invest in areas such as arms and tobacco, oil or pharmaceuticals. But not everyone has the same views on what makes an ethical or environmentally friendly fund. While some investors prefer to avoid companies they view as 'bad guys', others take the positive approach of picking companies that are making an active contribution to society or the environment such as those who specialise in recycling waste or the manufacture of wind power generators. Public transport groups and cycle manufacturers would also make the grade in this type of portfolio as would companies that spend large amounts on supporting community projects.

If you want an independent financial adviser who specialises in this sector, contact the Ethical Investment Research Service on 020 7840 5700 or visit its website at *www.eiris.org*.

How to save

So you have decided a collective fund is right for you and know which one you want. But should you save monthly or invest a lump sum? The decision will partly depend on whether you have a lump sum to spare or can only afford to make small monthly payments.

The danger of investing a lump sum is that the stock market may collapse just after you make your investment and it may take a long time for you to recover your losses, never mind seeing the money make a profit.

If you are worried about getting the timing wrong, then you can reduce your risk by making regular small contributions rather than a single large lump sum investment. This is called 'drip feeding'. The disadvantage of this approach is that if the fund rises steadily in value during the period, you will have missed out on much of the profit you would have got if you had simply invested a lump sum and left it to grow.

The advantage is that if the fund is volatile, you may get more units for your money one month than you do the next, therefore smoothing out the impact of any market fluctuations.

Savings plans

Unit Trust and Investment Trust groups offer monthly savings schemes that are pretty flexible.

If you want to stop contributions or increase or decrease them at any time, then you can, so long as you stick to the fund group's rules on minimum investment levels. You can also cash your investment in at any time if you need the money. But what you will get back will depend on the prices of the units or shares at that time.

Final pot

Your choice between making lump sum or regular savings will affect the final size of your investment pot.

According to figures from the Investment Management Association, based on research by performance monitoring group Reuters Lipper Hindsight, a lump sum investment of £1,000 in the average UK All Companies Unit Trust (a growth fund) 10 years ago would have grown to £2,246 by 28 September 2001 so long as the net income was reinvested.

Over the same period a £50 a month regular investment would have grown to £8,113.

According to the Association of Investment Trust Companies, a £1,000 lump sum in the average UK growth fund would have grown to £2,944 and a £50 a month regular investment to £10,522 over 10 years.

Compare both sets of figures to a £1,000 investment in a typical instant access building society savings account. It would have grown to just £1,335 over the same period and a £50 a month investment into the same account would have grown to around £6,830.

Time on your side

Collective funds can be an ideal way for a parent, grandparent or godparent to save for a child's future. The big advantage of saving for children is the investment period you have at your disposal. You have time to recover from any damaging dips in the stock market. From birth to 18 or 21 is a generous period for any investment and it should grow into a useful sum that can be put towards any of the big costs associated with a child's first steps into adulthood.

Child benefit as an investment

As discussed in Chapter 1, all families receive child benefit for their children. If they can afford to do so, many parents like to earmark the weekly payments for building an investment for their children's future.

Kid-friendly plans

Many fund groups like to promote the benefits of saving for the younger generation and you can choose any fund you like that suits your investment goals.

A few organisations go one step further and package their savings plans specifically for the children's market. These plans aim to attract the attention of adults who are looking for a way to invest for their offspring but find it hard to pick from the huge choice of funds available. Such packages also aim to make investing more fun for children and encourage them to take an interest in how the investment process works.

Lasting appeal

These plans can also provide an interesting alternative for relatives or godparents who want to give children a birthday or Christmas present with more lasting appeal than a battery-operated robot dog or a pack of Pokémon cards. An adult must set up the scheme but it can be designated in the child's initials or name and transferred fully into his or her name at the age of 18.

Unit Trusts for kids

Of the Unit Trusts directly targeting the children's market, the most well established plan is Invesco Perpetual's Rupert Fund. The scheme accepts regular monthly payments by direct debit from £20 or lump sums from £50. Other regular payments can be set up, such as annually at Christmas or a birthday from £50 by direct debit. In the 10 years to the end of September 2001, a £1,000 investment rose in value to over £2,000, with net income reinvested, according to *Money Management* magazine.

The group offers a Rupert Bear birthday card for youngsters up to the age of 11 and it also runs a children's page on its website.

A more recent player in the market is Aberdeen's Thomas and Friends investment plan, launched in autumn 2001. The plan allows the purchasing adult to choose from one or all of three Unit Trusts managed by Aberdeen that offer different levels of risk. There is a low-risk corporate bond fund, a medium-risk blue chip fund and a higher-risk international fund. The minimum investment on behalf of a child is £25 a month or £400 for a lump sum. Children receive a certificate featuring a picture of Thomas the Tank Engine.

Investment Trusts for kids

Relatives preferring an Investment Trust fund have two main schemes to consider. One is Witan's *Jump* plan that gives investors access to global stock markets through the Witan Investment Trust, one of the biggest and oldest Investment Trusts. It is a global growth fund managed by Henderson Global Investors, a UK investment group. The Witan trust invests in a wide range of shares and securities from across the world, including the UK. In the 10 years to the end of September 2001, £1,000 invested would have trebled to over £3,000 assuming the net income was reinvested.

James Budden, marketing manager of Witan Investment Trust, says: 'One of the key advantages of an Investment Trust over a Unit Trust is the fact there are no annual charges. Over a long period an annual charge of one per cent does add up. Another benefit is that being a closed-ended fund, an Investment

Trust is not under any pressure to meet redemptions if there is a sudden increase in sellers. That can cause increased volatility.'

He also points to gearing as being another advantage for Investment Trusts. He says: 'Gearing allows the trust assets to work harder especially in a rising market. But it can go the other way when a market falls.'

An adult can start a *Jump* plan on behalf of a child with either a minimum regular direct debit contribution from £25 or a lump sum from £100.

The other main Investment Trust scheme directed at kids is Edinburgh Fund Managers' InvestIT for Children plan. The plan is essentially its standard savings plan relabelled for children. It offers access to around 15 Investment Trusts on a minimum investment of £20 a month or a £150 lump sum.

In whose name?

As with shares, it is normally not possible for young children to take out a collective fund in their own name.

Some fund managers do allow children aged 14 and above to hold investments in their own names, so long as all the income is reinvested and they do not cash in any of the investment until they are at least 18. However, it is more usual for an investment to be registered in the name of the adult who buys it. The adult can then designate it in the child's name. For example, if the Fairy Godmother wanted to take out a plan for Cinderella, she could open an account Fairy Godmother a/c Cinderella (or simply 'C'), on behalf of her goddaughter. This is an informal way of stating that the investment is held on Cinderella's behalf.

The Fairy Godmother would be the only person recognised by the fund manager, and, as the legal owner, would also be free to sell the investment if she wanted to.

Bare trusts

A more formal arrangement worth considering is to set up a bare trust that makes life easier when the child turns 18. Otherwise it can be a hassle to arrange the transfer of the investment. A bare trust is a simple legal document that records the fact that the investor has taken out the plan on behalf of the child. The adult does not control the investment or any income from it; it cannot be used by either the adult or the child but must be left to build up.

Tax issues

If you are a grandparent or godparent buying the investment on behalf of a child then any income will be treated as if it is the child's and is taxed accordingly.

As all children have an annual income tax allowance (£4,615 for the 2002–2003 tax year), it is extremely unlikely for them to face a tax bill unless they have a large number of lucrative income-generating investments or an excessively well-paid paper round!

As mentioned in earlier chapters, if you are a parent making the investment and the annual income exceeds £100 a year, it's a different story. All the income will be taxed as if it is your own income (£200 for two parents). Because of this potential income tax hassle, it can make sense to consider buying investment funds that concentrate on growth rather than income.

Capital gains tax

The whole point of investing for your children's future is to try and build up a fund larger than the one you started with. All being well, the investment will result in a capital gain when it is finally sold. It is unlikely your child will face a tax bill as a result because all children have the same annual Capital Gains Tax (CGT) exemption as adults (£7,700 in the 2002–2003 tax year).

If the investment gains do exceed the exemption, then CGT will be charged at the child's top rate of tax. However, the rate of CGT is tapered over 10 years so that the tax reduces the longer the investment is held.

There are also potential inheritance tax implications for adults investing on behalf of children. They are described in more detail in Chapter 13.

How to buy

If you are confident enough to make your own investment decisions you can buy Unit Trusts and OEICs directly from the fund group of your choice. However, it is normally cheaper to go through a discount broker or a fund supermarket because they offer discounts on initial charges and commission.

Buying Investment Trusts

For Investment Trusts you need to use a stockbroker, independent adviser or an execution-only share dealing service. If you want to start a savings plan you can contact the Investment Trust group direct.

For details on Investment Trusts, contact The Association of Investment Trust Companies (AITC) on 020 7282 5555 or visit its website at *www.aitc.co.uk*. To find a traditional stockbroker or execution-only service try the Association of Private Client Investment Managers and Stockbrokers at *www.apcims.co.uk*.

Independent advice

It can be hard to decide which is the right fund for you, particularly if you are a first-time investor. If you're struggling with the choice you should seek independent financial advice. You can pick either a commission-based firm of independent financial advisers that will usually be paid commission taken from any investment you buy, or a fee-based adviser, in which case you will pay him or her a fee for the advice you get.

Some independent financial advisers offer a mixture of the two charging structures.

Finding an adviser

A good way to find a suitable adviser is to ask a friend, family member or work colleague if they can recommend one. If that route fails you can find one by calling the Unit Trust Information Service on 020 8207 1361. Alternatively phone Independent Financial Adviser Promotion on 0117 971 1177 or visit *www.unbiased.co.uk*. Also consider the Institute of Financial Planning on 0117 945 2470 (*www.financialplanning.org.uk*) or the Society of Financial Advisers on 020 8989 8464 (*www.sofa.org*).

Keep track

Once you have made any investment, do not just stick the paperwork in the drawer and forget about it. It is essential to keep an eye on how the investment is performing. You will receive statements and annual reports to help you monitor whether they are on track to meet your savings goals – don't just throw them in the bin without looking at them.

Remember to watch the newspapers both for price performance information and for any stories on the financial pages that may be relevant to your fund.

7

Tax-free equity investments

'The best things in life are free.'

Proverb

The government is keen for more of us to start saving up for our own and our children's futures. It knows that it must offer incentives, however, or else we just won't do it.

One of the favourite carrots dangled by successive governments is to let us save tax-free. *Tax-free* is music to investors' ears. After all, it is one of life's financial injustices that we carefully save money out of our taxed income, only to see any returns on those savings taxed as well.

Chapter 4 examined tax-friendly cash investments. But there are also plenty of opportunities to shelter shares and investment funds (and their potentially greater returns) using equity Individual Savings Accounts (ISAs) and Personal Equity Plans (PEPs).

PEPs

PEPs were introduced in January 1987 to encourage wider share ownership by individuals. The rules for investment limits were low at the start but after a few years allowed you to invest up to

£6,000 in a general PEP plus a further £3,000 in a single company PEP each tax year until April 1999, when PEPs were replaced by ISAs. By sheltering these investments in a PEP, there was no tax to pay on any dividends and no Capital Gains Tax on any growth in value.

PEPs proved a massive hit and tens of billions of pounds poured into the plans and although ISAs replaced them, investors can continue holding their PEP plans and let them grow with the same tax breaks. The only difference to the original tax rules is that the dividend tax credit of 10 per cent on ordinary shares and some Unit Trusts held in a PEP, as with ISAs, can only be reclaimed up to 5 April 2004.

Relaxed rules

Not only can investors enjoy most of the same tax breaks on their old PEPs, but they can also do more with the money they hold in them. In April 2001, the investment rules surrounding PEPs were relaxed and brought into line with ISAs.

Although you can no longer put new money into a PEP plan, you can make your PEP investments work harder for you by taking advantage of the more flexible environment. Under the old regime a general PEP fund had to be more than 50 per cent invested in the UK and continental Europe. This means that people who took out a PEP when they were introduced and bought one every year until 1999 could be sitting on a very tidy sum indeed. However, that portfolio is likely to be heavily skewed towards the UK and the rest of Europe and may benefit from some balancing.

Although you have always been able to transfer PEPs from one provider to another if dissatisfied with performance, the funds you could move to were also restricted by the old PEP investment rules. Now PEP holders can switch the contents of their PEPs to different types of funds, enabling them to create a potentially more exciting or at least a balanced mix of investments.

Under the new rules, single company PEPs, with their exposure to the fortunes, good or bad, of just one company (like BT or Marks and Spencer), can now be cashed in and the money transferred to a general plan without the tax break being lost. So if you are lucky enough to have built up a PEP portfolio, you can start using it more effectively to save for your children's future.

Depending on your attitude to risk and how much time there is before you or your offspring need the money, you could think about a PEP overhaul.

Transfer costs

If you decide to refresh your PEP collection there will be costs involved. There may be exit charges to pay on the old funds plus initial charges on the new. Watch out for financial advisers who approach you out of the blue with an offer to review your PEP holdings, especially if they were the ones who sold you the PEPs the first time round and then failed to give ongoing advice. They are probably just interested in the large commissions a transfer might generate.

Fund supermarkets

If you know what you want in terms of new funds and are prepared to do the switching yourself, then a discount broker or one of the new breed of on-line fund supermarkets are probably your cheapest options. However, be aware that you can only switch Unit Trust and OEIC PEPs this way. If your PEPs were concentrated in Investment Trusts you will need to use a stockbroker or independent financial adviser (see Chapter 6 for more details).

Not all supermarkets offer PEP transfers and those that do will not necessarily offer access to the funds you want. Make sure you do your research first and then pick the supermarket that offers the best deal for your chosen funds. Some supermarkets you can use yourself, such as *www.fundsnetwork.co.uk* and *www.egg.com*. Others, such as Cofunds, are used only by financial advisers. Some advisers have access to more than one supermarket and may offer you further discounts.

To find an independent financial adviser, contact IFA Promotion on 0117 971 1177 (*www.unbiased.co.uk*), the Society of Financial Advisers (Sofa) on 020 8989 8464 (*www.sofa.org*)

or the Institute of Financial Planning on 0117 945 2470 (*www.financialplanning.org.uk*).

Equity ISAs

ISAs were introduced in April 1999 to replace Personal Equity Plans. Anyone over the age of 18 and resident in the UK can take out a plan and use it to shelter shares or funds up to a maximum value of £7,000 each tax year.

ISAs come in two main forms: a maxi or a mini plan.

Maxi plans

With a maxi ISA you can either combine three elements: cash, equities and life assurance, with your annual allowance split into £3,000, £3,000 and £1,000 respectively. Or alternatively, you can invest the whole £7,000 in a maxi plan devoted to equities.

You can choose to save on a regular basis or invest a lump sum.

Mini plans

If you take the mini route, you can take out a mini plan for each of the three classes of investment. The split between the classes of investment is the same: so £3,000 for cash, £3,000 for equities and £1,000 for insurance.

Equity options

With equity plans, either mini or maxi, you can choose to buy funds using a general plan or you can pick your own shares through a so-called 'self-select' ISA. If you want a self-select plan, you have to open either a mini or maxi ISA account with a stockbroker and buy and sell shares in the normal way up to the maximum annual allowance.

Doubling up

You are not allowed to hold a maxi and a mini in a single tax year. So, if you have already taken out a mini cash ISA, or are considering taking one out in the current tax year, then you are restricted to taking a mini plan for your equity investment.

Future saving

The good news is that ISAs will be around for several more years. Plus the government has agreed to maintain the current investment limits at least until 2005. So let's say you start to save using ISAs for the first time from the tax year beginning April 2002. That means you have at least four years ahead in which you can make stock market investments tax-free. The total you can save is £28,000 in a series of maxi plans or £12,000 in mini plans, or you can mix the different types over the years.

Tax-free warning

One of the golden rules of investment is not to get too carried away by the tax-free tag. There's an old saying used by wise financial advisers that you should not let the tax tail wag the investment dog. If your investment does not earn any income or the capital fails to grow there would be no tax to pay anyway. And there are usually management charges for ISA plans to add into the equation.

ISAs and PEPs are simply tax-free wrappers around existing equity investments. The underlying investments will be hit just as hard by any stock market volatility as those outside tax-free shelters. And remember, the 10 per cent dividend tax credit cannot be retained after 5 April 2004.

Buying ISAs

You can buy ISAs through discount brokers, fund supermarkets and independent financial advisers as mentioned for PEPs.

CAT marks

When ISAs were launched the government introduced so-called CAT standards. CAT stands for Charges, Access and Terms. It is a voluntary standard devised by the government that some providers apply to their plans but it is no guarantee of how well the ISA will perform.

A CAT marked equity ISA must charge no more than one per cent a year and apply no other charges. It must also allow minimum savings of no more than £50 a month or £500 a year.

In the case of Unit Trusts and OEICs, at least 50 per cent of the fund must be in eligible European listed shares and securities. For both Unit Trusts and OEICs, the buying and selling prices of units must be the same.

For more information on ISAs, contact the Unit Trust Information Service on 020 8207 1361 or visit the Investment Management Association website at *www.investmentuk.org*

8

Halfway houses

'A middle course is the safest for you to take.'

Ovid, *Metamorphoses* (between 43 BC and AD 17)

Investing for your children's future is not just about choosing between low-risk cash deposits and high-risk equities. There is a range of halfway house alternatives that offer the chance to produce decent returns without investors exposing themselves to a high degree of risk. Such medium-risk investments include gilts, corporate bonds and with-profits bonds and endowments.

Gilts

Gilts, short for gilt-edged securities, are loans made to the government by investors. In return for the cash, which is used for public spending, they receive a bond that pays a set amount of interest, called a coupon, twice a year.

They have been around since 1694 when the government launched the first gilt to raise cash to help fund a war with France.

Around £300 billion is invested in gilts, £35 billion belonging to private investors.

As with equities, gilts have good years and bad years, the year 2000 being an excellent one. While stock market investors saw their returns fall 8.6 per cent over the year, gilt investors were toasting investment returns of more than 6 per cent, according to the 2001 Barclays Capital Equity-Gilt study.

Sturdy performance

Over the last decade gilts have proved sturdy performers. The average total return (combined income and capital growth) was 9.4 per cent a year compared with equities at 11.8 per cent a year over the same period – but equities have a greater exposure to risk.

You cannot guarantee that gilts will always be reliable performers, however. In the 1960s, 1970s and 1980s, average annual returns were negative while equity values increased. And over the long-term they are definitely second best when compared with shares. Had your great-great grandfather invested £100 in gilts in 1899 and reinvested the income, it would have been worth just £289 by the end of 2000. The same amount invested in shares would have grown to £22,817.

Barclays research also shows how important it is to reinvest income if you can. Had your great-great grandfather neglected to reinvest the income, the returns by 2000 would have been a paltry £1 for gilts and £253 for shares.

Gilts tend to do better in a low-inflation environment. Runaway inflation is bad because as inflation rises so do interest rates, but the coupons on gilts remain the same.

Which gilt?

Gilts come in three types: dated, undated and convertible. Dated gilts promise to pay you a fixed amount on a set date in the future. Undated gilts have no set redemption date, and may never be redeemed, while convertibles allow you to switch to a better deal once a year.

The dated gilts come in three groups: short-dated, medium-dated and long-dated. The *Financial Times* defines short-dated gilts as those with a redemption within five years and the Stock Exchange says seven years.

For medium-dated gilts the redemption dates are within five or seven to 15 years. Long-dated gilts have redemption dates more than 15 years away.

The values of longer-dated gilts tend to be more volatile than shorter-dated gilts.

Safe haven

The big attraction of gilts is that they are a safe haven for cautious investors because there is little chance of the government defaulting on the loans.

And because most gilts, which are split into units with a face value of £100, carry a redemption date when the loan is repaid, you can work out what the capital return is likely to be. It is possible to calculate the overall return, including the income, by looking at the redemption yield. You can work it out yourself, but several newspapers will include the redemption yield in the gilt listings.

You are not obliged to hold gilts until the repayment date as you can sell them at any time. What you get will depend on the prevailing price.

Any capital gain on gilts is also tax-free and losses cannot be offset against capital losses made on other investments.

Future goals

If you have a particular date in mind for handing a cash sum to your kids, say to help them survive the lean university years in 15 years' time, or fund a first car when they are 18, then you could think about finding a gilt or series of gilts with redemption dates to match.

You should concentrate on gilts that offer the best after-tax redemption yield for your tax position. As a rule of thumb, a top-rate taxpayer should consider low-coupon gilts and non-taxpayers high-coupon gilts. Income from gilts is paid gross, but taxpayers will still need to pay tax on that income through their self-assessment tax return.

Index-linked

If you are concerned that inflation may rear its head again, you can opt for an index-linked gilt. These have very low fixed rates of interest but do compensate you for the effects of inflation.

Totally tax-free

You can shelter gilts from income tax by putting them in a self-select Individual Savings Account – up to £3,000 a year in a mini stocks and shares ISA or up to £7,000 in a maxi ISA. However, they must have redemption dates of five years or more to qualify.

Buying gilts

Investors can buy new issues of gilts direct from the government through the Debt Management Office for a minimum application of £1,000. Information is available on its website, *www.dmo.gov.uk*. The site includes daily gilt price listings. Prices are also published in several national daily newspapers.

You can trade gilts using a form available from post offices or by phoning the Bank of England Registrars Department (01452 398333). Commission is charged at 0.7 per cent (minimum £12.50) for purchases up to £5,000. If you buy more than £5,000 you pay £35 plus 0.375 per cent for any amount over £5,000. (There is no minimum commission on a sale.) You can also trade through a stockbroker or bank at their commission rates. Unless you are confident about what you are doing, you should always seek independent financial advice before buying.

Corporate bonds

It is not only the government that likes to borrow money from the public. Companies do too. In return for your money, normally used to invest in the business, the companies issue corporate bonds.

As with gilts, companies pay bond investors interest on their money. The bonds also have a maturity date and normally pay the coupon in twice-yearly parts. Because no company can guarantee that it will not go bust, the interest paid on the bonds is generally higher than on gilts.

Corporate bonds are considered to be less risky than if you bought shares in the same company. This is because a collapsed company must pay all its debts first, including to bondholders, before compensating any shareholders. They can therefore suit parents with a more cautious attitude to investing for their children.

Bonds come in different grades and pay different rates of

interest, depending on the risk associated with the companies issuing them. They are rated by independent credit rating agencies such as Standard & Poor's or Moody's. Higher ratings mean the bonds are 'investment-grade', and so are considered lower risk. Investors opting for lower grade, or 'non-investment grade' bonds, will receive higher rates of interest to compensate for the extra risk. But even if you pick bonds with a high rating, there is no guarantee that they will remain highly rated. As with shares, you need to monitor the ratings and keep a look out for stories in the financial pages about how the company is performing.

Buying corporate bonds

You can buy corporate bonds directly through a stockbroker. But the same risks apply to buying single bonds as to investing in single shares. If you buy just one or two bonds, you are taking a huge risk with your money, whereas if you have plenty of cash to invest, then you can spread the risk among many bonds. A lower cost route into bond investing is through a bond fund, such as a Unit Trust, OEIC or Investment Trust that invests in a large portfolio of bonds. There are many funds to choose from.

There are two main types of fund: corporate bond funds and high-yield funds.

Corporate bond funds aim to offer a yield higher than you would get from deposit accounts, while high-yield funds aim for a higher return.

Managers of corporate bond funds tend to buy investment grade bonds while the high-yield fund managers will buy at least a proportion of the more risky bonds to help them achieve a higher income.

The yields on bonds are not guaranteed and are affected by general movements in interest rates. The fund manager has to try to protect against this by investing in a broad range of bonds with different redemption dates. You also need to be aware that capital is not guaranteed and can fluctuate in value.

Growth options

Corporate bond funds are normally preferred by investors looking for income. They pay out at regular intervals such as monthly, quarterly, half yearly or yearly. But if you are a cautious investor, you can use them for capital growth instead by re-investing the income.

The income from corporate bond funds is taxable and is paid net of lower-rate tax. The way income from corporate bond funds is treated depends on whether the income is distributed as interest or a dividend. Unit Trusts and OEICs investing more than 60 per cent of their assets in gilts, corporate bonds or cash pay interest; funds investing mostly in UK or foreign shares pay dividends. Tax credits on dividend distributions can be reclaimed if the fund is held within an equity ISA up to 5 April 2004.

Outside an ISA non-taxpayers can reclaim the tax but higher-rate taxpayers will have to pay the difference through their tax return. Any capital gain will be subject to tax if it exceeds the annual CGT exemption, currently £7,700.

Charges

Another point to watch with corporate bond funds is that initial charges and annual management fees can nibble away at your returns. Some funds take charges from the income and others from the capital. Most investment experts prefer to see the charges taken from income so that your capital is not eaten away simply to maintain a high level of income.

With-profits bonds and endowments

Alternative halfway house options for investors are plans based around with-profits funds.

However if you have been reading the financial pages of newspapers over the last year or two you might be questioning the wisdom of investing in with-profits bonds. They have been criticised for several reasons, including their complicated structures, the high commissions taken by salesmen and the lack of transparency regarding charges. But they still have a role to play in many investors' portfolios.

Endowments, which are with-profits plans with life insurance attached, took a public battering when warnings were issued that many would not meet targets for investors who took them out to support interest-only mortgages. (See Main risks, below.)

How they work

With-profits investments are policies offered by insurance companies where investors' monthly or lump sum investments are pooled into a single pot. The fund managers then use that money to buy a mixture of investments ranging from property and shares to cash and fixed-interest securities such as gilts and corporate bonds. Over the term of the policy, the returns you receive should reflect the overall growth of the fund. Endowment plans tend to run for longer periods, typically 25 years if linked to a mortgage, and include life insurance.

Smoothing effect

Both these types of investment have been considered safe havens for investors in the past because they promise to pay regular annual bonuses whatever the state of the stock market. This is known as the 'smoothing effect'.

To be able to do this, fund managers hold back some of the returns made in the good years so that they can afford to pay bonuses in the lean years. Once a bonus has been announced it cannot be taken away, even if the market falls dramatically, so long as you keep a policy going for a minimum term.

Investors also receive a 'terminal bonus' when the bond is cashed in. You normally only receive this if you have held the bond for at least five years. The longer you hold the bond, the higher the terminal bonus should be.

According to Jason Hollands of the London-based independent investment advisers Bestinvest, with-profits returns should not be compared to stock market performance even though much of the underlying investment is in equities. He says: 'These are low risk investments and should be compared with deposits or National Savings. In this context they remain attractive.'

Income tax

With-profits bonds are not suitable for everyone, according to

Hollands: 'For starters, basic-rate tax is automatically deducted from them and cannot be reclaimed so they are not ideal for non-taxpayers. Top-rate taxpayers may have to pay extra tax through their income tax returns.'

Another pitfall is the early exit penalties, which make the bonds unsuitable for investors who cannot tie their money up for a minimum of five years.

But Hollands believes they suit cautious, medium-term investors who want a steady annual return. He adds: 'They may also appeal to those who already use their full ISA allowances and Capital Gains Tax allowance because there is no Capital Gains Tax to pay when they are cashed in.

He says: 'Higher-rate tax payers whose rate is expected to fall in the future, say on retirement, may benefit. The bonds only incur income tax in the year you cash them in or withdraw money in excess of five per cent a year.'

Main risks

As mentioned above in the introduction, the spotlight has been on with-profits over the last couple of years. As well as the criticisms already described, there has also been a trend of falling bonuses because weak stock market performance during 2000 and 2001 eroded many insurance companies' reserves. This made them nervous about paying out attractive bonuses.

The problems at Equitable Life did not help. The troubled life insurer had not built up enough reserves to pay promised guarantees to certain pension customers. The crisis led the Department of Trade and Industry to demand that with-profits funds must always hold back enough reserves to meet the agreed bonuses. This meant insurers with low reserves were forced to hold a bigger percentage of low-risk investments such as gilts, inevitably affecting a bond's performance.

Where to go for help

It can be hard for investors to be sure they have got a good deal on a with-profits investment because it is difficult to compare performance. One thing is sure, you need to consider the financial strength of the provider and work out the impact of the charges.

For example, with-profits bonds that promise high annual bonuses may be taking bigger annual charges, or may simply offer a high rate in the early years that will drop off later.

If you cannot decide on the bond you want, it is a good idea to take independent financial advice. Good sources of independent information include Bestinvest in London and Baronworth Investment Services based in Ilford, Essex. *Money Management* also publishes surveys on the sector.

Second-hand endowments

Endowment plans are often started up by savers who later decide they do not want or cannot afford to keep them going. Just one in three policies makes it to maturity. Many people simply cancel the plans or surrender them to the insurance company, but another option is to sell them on the second-hand market, where you are likely to get more than you would by surrendering them.

Why buy someone else's endowment?

Buying a second-hand endowment is considered a relatively attractive investment for a low-risk investor. The advantage is that the original policyholder has already paid all the setting up costs of the policy and you simply buy the plan at the prevailing price and continue to pay the monthly premiums until the plan matures. When it matures you should get a terminal bonus that may be as much as 50 per cent of the value of the policy.

However, the disadvantage of a second-hand plan is that the policy will pay out on the death of the original policyholder if that is before maturity. That may be inconvenient for you in terms of timing, particularly for your tax planning. You may also be liable for Capital Gains Tax if the increased value exceeds your annual allowance. There is also a risk, as with most investments, that the endowment may not perform to your expectations.

You can buy a policy either at auction or from a market maker. For more information about second-hand endowments, contact the Association of Policy Market Makers on 020 7739 3949 or visit *www.apmm.org*.

9

Stakeholder pensions

'Old age is the most unexpected of all the things that happen to a man.'

Leon Trotsky, 18 May 1935, from his *Diary in Exile*

Parents or grandparents who want to pass money to the younger generation but are concerned that the latter may blow the inheritance at a young age have a new option to consider: a pension. Dull as it may seem to a child, who believes old age is an infinite time away, a pension is a tax-efficient, long-term investment that he or she may well be grateful for when retirement looms closer.

It is only recently that parents could even consider pensions as part of their investment strategy for children, thanks to the arrival of stakeholder pensions in April 2001.

Pension scandals

Big changes are now underway in the pensions market after years of turmoil that deterred many people from making provision for their retirement.

First there was the Maxwell scandal in the early 1990s that

shook the company pensions sector.

Then there was the personal pensions mis-selling scandal where thousands of people were persuaded by unscrupulous pensions salesmen to transfer out of top quality occupational schemes into personal plans. More recently, the Equitable Life furore over guaranteed pensions and the demise of several employer final salary schemes has added to investor nervousness.

But headline-grabbing developments were not the only cause for concern: pensions also developed a bad name for their confusing terminology, high charges and inflexible terms. The rules were also so rigid that only working people could pay into plans. If a woman took time off work to bring up a family she had to halt pension payments. If a worker was unemployed for a time, the pension suffered again.

And the hassle and cost of switching plans prevented pension holders from making sure they had the right deal.

High charges

Overall costs also hampered the image of personal pensions. It was not unusual for investors to see up to two years' contributions swallowed up in charges and commissions before their pension money started working for them.

Flexible plans

The government had to act quickly to sort out this diverse and damaging range of pension problems. It had to do something urgent to encourage people to make their own pension provision because the state could no longer promise to provide pensions at the same level in the future for the growing numbers of pensioners.

Birth of Stakeholder

In the late 1990s, the government carried out a review of pensions in the UK that resulted in new legislation in 2001. At the centre of the new laws was the introduction of the Stakeholder pension, a government-devised, flexible, simple to understand and low-cost pension plan for the masses.

Stakeholder plans were launched in April 2001 with the chief aim of encouraging low earners and those without any pension provision, such as the self-employed, to start saving for their retirement for the first time.

What is a Stakeholder plan?

To be recognised as a Stakeholder pension, a plan must allow a minimum contribution of £20 or less, make a single annual charge of no more than one per cent (unless the investor wants extra advice) and charge no penalties for switching to another Stakeholder or for stopping or restarting the plan.

Apart from these core definitions, Stakeholder rules are the same as for personal pensions. For example, you can choose to take your pension income at any time from between the age of 50 and 75, and when you do you can opt to use the whole pot to buy an income (called an annuity) or take up to 25 per cent of the fund as tax-free cash and use the rest to produce a smaller income.

There are also different options for the type of income you take, such as choosing an income fixed for life or one that increases in line with inflation. You have the right to use part of the fund for an income and leave the rest invested, although under current rules you must buy an annuity by the time you are 75.

Positive side effects

One welcome change triggered by Stakeholder was that it forced pension companies to be more competitive on charges, with the cost of many traditional plans falling since Stakeholder was announced. So even if you do not take out a Stakeholder plan, an old-fashioned plan ought to be cheaper than before.

Wider market

So what does all this mean for saving for your offspring? Well, another big change introduced by Stakeholder is that for the first time, pension plans can be taken out by non-earners. So non-working spouses and workers who stop earning through no fault of their own such as through redundancy or ill-health can take out plans using savings or money from their partner.

In fact, anyone up to the age of 75 has an annual Stakeholder allowance regardless of whether or not he or she earns an income – and that includes children.

Stakeholders effect on children

The only restriction under Stakeholder is that non-earners, such as children, may only invest a maximum of £2,808 each tax year. The government tops that up with basic-rate tax relief to £3,600. If you are an earner, however, you can pay more than this depending on the level of your annual earning, but ranging from 17.5 per cent for those aged up to 35 to 40 per cent for those aged 61 and above, subject to a maximum earnings cap of £97,200 in the tax year 2002–2003.

London-based stockbroker Killik & Co launched a Stakeholder plan in 2001 in conjunction with Scottish Widows very much with an eye on the children's market. It calculated that a parent or grandparent's investment of a single annual allowance of £2,808 at birth, plus the government top-up, would produce a retirement pot of £128,000 by the time the child reached 60, even if no more was added. This is assuming annual growth of seven per cent.

If the full allowance was paid every year until the child reached the age of 60, he or she could be looking at a mammoth £3.1 million pension fund, again assuming annual growth of seven per cent, according to Killik.

Child benefit

Philippa Gee, a financial adviser at Torquil Clark, an independent pensions adviser based in Wolverhampton, West Midlands, says parents can build up a decent pension pot for their kids simply by diverting child benefit payments into a Stakeholder plan.

She says: 'It is an excellent kick-start for a child's pension and doesn't cost parents a penny. The weekly child benefit contribution for the eldest child is £15.50 and is automatically worth an extra 22 per cent when you add in the tax relief given on Stakeholder.

'And by doing that from birth until age 18 and leaving the fund to roll up without any further contributions, the pot could be worth over £500,000, assuming annual growth rates of seven per cent.'

Your children may not like it but the earliest they can get their hands on the pension is when they reach 50. And under the current rules, only 25 per cent of the fund may be turned into cash.

Which pension?

You don't have to pick a pure Stakeholder plan if you don't want to. Some personal pensions outside the Stakeholder stable will accept children. Just ask the provider of the plan you are interested in.

The advantage of a Stakeholder plan over alternatives is that it offers guarantees on costs and flexibility that may not apply to other personal pension plans.

Which funds?

The message about any investment for children is that you have time on your side. The more time you have to invest, the more risks you can afford to take. When it comes to a pension plan, you have even longer than for the usual children's investments – as much as 50 years or more.

Compound growth

Gordon Maw of Virgin Direct says around 15 per cent of the Stakeholder plans the company sold within the first six months of Stakeholder's launch were for children. He says: 'There are two golden rules in financial planning. The first is always to use every available tax break. The second is to make compound interest do the hard work for you. Paying into a pension for a child appeals because a pension is the UK's last great tax loophole. Better still, compound growth over that kind of period really is the investor's best friend, making every £1 you invest many times more productive.'

Making choices

There are dozens of Stakeholder plans to choose from, although it has to be said that, the rules capping charges at one per cent a year have meant many companies fear they would never see a profit and so have pulled out of the market.

Because the charges are similar between Stakeholder plans, you need to look at the underlying funds on offer before making the final choice of scheme. However, the principles surrounding the choice of a Stakeholder are the same as for any other investments, although you have more time to ride the ups and downs of the stock market.

The funds you pick will depend on whether you have a steady-eddy approach to investing or are more gung-ho and are prepared to take big risks.

The types of funds on offer under Stakeholder vary from provider to provider. So always check first whether you are happy with the menu available.

With so much time to play with, you can take a bit more risk with the investment in the early years – but only if you want to. It will be up to your child or grandchild to take over the investment decisions when they reach adulthood.

'Default' option

If you have chosen your provider but cannot make up your mind about which fund is the most appropriate or do not want to make a decision, then the pension company will put your money into a 'default' fund. The default option will usually be a managed fund that invests in a wide range of UK and international equities with the aim of steady growth.

Anecdotal evidence suggests that most parents and grandparents investing in a Stakeholder prefer to take the default option.

If you decide to be more active with your offspring's Stakeholder, then you may want a Stakeholder with a wide choice of funds to pick from. Most providers will let you switch from fund to fund for a small cost. So you could start off with a high-risk approach using a specialist fund such as one specialising in the Far East or in technology and later on switch to a managed fund or even a lower-risk cash and bond fund. If in doubt about what to do, you should always speak to an independent financial adviser.

Performance figures

But how do you pick the right fund? There is no simple answer, unfortunately. There has been much debate about investors relying too heavily on past performance tables, especially when they make their decisions based on figures used in advertising by financial companies. Traditionally, the message has been 'past performance is no guarantee of future performance'.

But in autumn 2001, the financial watchdog the Financial Services Authority (FSA) decided that it preferred the wording 'past performance is no guide to future performance'. This makes life hard for investors. In a bid to help them through the maze, the FSA has introduced a range of league tables that compare financial products, but they specifically exclude past performance (visit *www.fsa.gov.uk/tables*).

Past and present

Despite the debate, it is a sensible exercise to look at how your chosen fund or funds have behaved in the past. You need to look for consistency over many years and not just pick a fund that is a top performer in the last year or two, for example. You also need to keep a look out for any news about the fund group your chosen plan is invested with, including any changes to the individual managers of funds: such changes may have a big impact on the future performance.

Good sources of pension fund performance data include the monthly *Money Management* magazine available from newsagents, and *Moneyfacts Life and Pensions*, available on subscription from Moneyfacts, based in Norwich.

For general information about Stakeholder pensions, visit the Department of Work and Pensions special pension site at *www.pensionguide.gov.uk*.

10

School fees

'The roots of education are bitter but the fruits are sweet.'

Aristotle

Trainee wizard Harry Potter is one private school pupil who does not seem to worry who pays his school fees. Perhaps he has won a scholarship to Hogwart's school? Maybe he has enough cash stashed at the Gringotts bank to meet the costs? Or does he simply magic the problem away?

Unfortunately, ordinary people with no magic powers who want to send their offspring to fee-paying schools have to foot the bills themselves. Even people on modest incomes who are concerned about class sizes in the state sector are turning to private schools in larger numbers. Everyone knows that private education does not come cheap but many people get the fright of their lives when they see the size of the bills.

Average costs

According to recent research from the Independent Schools Council Information Service (ISCIS), the average cost of sending a child to a private boarding school is over £15,000 a year. Day schools are cheaper, but even they can dent your pocket by as much as £9,000 a year for the top schools, according to ISCIS figures.

A further sting in the tail is that school fees tend to rise faster than inflation. You need to bear that in mind when forecasting what your total bill will be. Experts reckon you should work out the sums on the basis that the fees will increase by at least five per cent a year.

The upshot is that if you want to send your children through the private sector all the way, you can expect to pay at least £200,000 apiece.

The financial agony does not end there. If your children go on to university after school, you can expect to fork out even more. Figures from the National Union of Students suggest it costs around £23,000 to put a student through a three-year course at university, taking into account tuition fees and living expenses. The government is investigating changes to the system that may reduce the financial pain for students and parents in years to come.

Time and cash poor

Unless you are well-off and can easily meet the costs out of income or have generous grandparents who want to help out (and reduce their potential inheritance tax liabilities, see Chapter 13) then your only options are to borrow or save.

If your first bill for school fees is looming and you cannot afford to pay from income, you will probably have to borrow the money. Relatives may be able to help, but it is likely the bank or building society will be your first port of call. Personal loans can be an expensive option and can be inflexible, although competition has increased in this sector in recent years and you may be able to find a deal that suits you.

Tony Brown of Clarke & Partners in Wimborne, Dorset, a school fees planning specialist, says: 'Most people would like to be able to plan ahead, but often they end up having to borrow. One of the most common ways is through re-mortgaging or using one of the new breed of flexible mortgages.'

Re-mortgaging is a popular option, especially for those whose homes have risen in value. You can release some of the equity built up in your property by re-mortgaging it for a higher amount. Competition between lenders means it may now be possible to borrow more money for a similar level of repayment. Shop around for the best deals on the internet or look at the personal finance sections of national newspapers for their best-buy tables.

Another good source of data on mortgage rates is Norwich-based Moneyfacts, an independent provider of financial information. It has a website at *www.moneyfacts.co.uk*. Alternatively, you can ask an independent mortgage broker for help, but you may have to pay for the service.

Flexible friend

Moving to a flexible mortgage may be another option to look at. There are a growing number of these loans available that let you draw down extra money when you need it. There are pre-set limits on how much you can borrow so that you remain on track to repay the debt.

Short-term saving

If you have up to five years in which to prepare your finances for the school-fees onslaught, you may think you have plenty of time to start saving. Unfortunately, five years is a short time in the investment world, and your options must realistically be restricted to cash or National Savings. Although the growth potential of cash and National Savings plans is not great, they are the safest homes for your money in the short term and you know it will be there when you come to write that first cheque.

You could consider taking out a cash ISA in which you can shelter up to £3,000 a year from the taxman. Parents can have one each, so between you, you can save up to £6,000 a year free of tax.

Cash ISAs offer some of the best savings rates around, especially when you consider interest on accounts held by taxpayers is taxed by at least 20 per cent, but they are not an option if you have already opened a maxi ISA for the same tax year. (For more details on cash and maxi ISAs, see Chapters 4 and 7.)

If you have already used up your ISA allowance or want to save more than £3,000 in cash, take a look at high interest internet or postal accounts from banks and building societies.

Long-term investing

For parents who have five to 10 years or more before facing that first set of fees, there are many more options for saving and for seeing those savings grow. Their best route to growth is through the stock market. Any equity related investment needs a good stretch of time to prove itself, but history shows it should pay off. According to figures from the Barclays annual Equity-Gilt survey, the average return from the stock market in the past 10 years has been 11.8 per cent a year for equities compared with 4.2 per cent for cash.

Independent investment adviser Bates Investment Services in Leeds calculates that parents hoping to send a child to private secondary school will have to put aside around £365 a month from birth in order to build up a big enough pot, assuming investment growth of seven per cent. If they put the moment off until the child is six then that figure leaps to £550 a month.

There are a wide range of investments to look at, depending on how much money you have to spare and your attitude to risk. You can choose to invest in a selection of single shares but to reduce the risk it may be better to consider a collective investment such as a Unit Trust, OEIC or Investment Trust instead (see Chapters 5 and 6.)

The more time you have until your deadline, the higher the risk you can take with the choice of funds, at least in the early years. You can switch to lower-risk funds later if necessary. But a few words of warning on all equity investments: there is no guarantee that you will meet your goals.

Tax-efficient investment on stock market

The most tax-efficient way to invest on the stock market is using your maximum £7,000 annual ISA allowance for a maxi ISA. You can either buy a self-select plan where you pick a selection of shares and/or funds to shelter or a scheme containing one or two funds. A couple can open one maxi ISA each, so with a maximum of £14,000 to salt away in an ISA, you could soon be on your way to building up a decent school fees fighting fund.

Remember, if you have already opened a cash ISA in any given tax year you will only be able to invest £3,000 in an equity ISA for that year, however.

Zero option

Another investment option that has been popular for the past 20 years among parents planning for school bills are zero dividend preference shares – known as zeros. These are one of the types of share linked to split-capital Investment Trusts. Investors wanting growth from their investment can choose 'capital shares', those wanting income can pick 'income shares' and those who want a known capital return can pick the zeros.

As their name suggests, zeros do not pay any income but they offer a fixed capital return on a set date in the future. The trusts are wound up on the set date and the assets are distributed, with zero holders first in line for payment. A series of individual zeros are often purchased by parents needing a sum on a particular date – such as the start of a new term.

They can be extremely tax-efficient as the only tax charged is on the capital gains. Well organised investors who make use of their annual Capital Gains Tax (CGT) exemption, can thus avoid tax altogether.

Zeros have been praised for being a solid investment because none had failed to pay out. But in the summer of 2001 concerns started to mount over whether some trusts might fall short. The problems arose because of the big growth in the number of split-capital Investment Trusts investing in the income and capital shares of other splits, which some experts condemned as highly risky. Many of the splits had borrowed heavily and faced the possibility of having to wind up the trust early if the banks called in their loans. Zero holders might be first in line for payouts among the shareholders, but unfortunately the banks, as lead creditors, get their money first.

Another problem for newer splits was their massive exposure to the technology sector that famously collapsed in spring 2001.

Some advisers believe there is still a place for zeros so long as investors are cautious about their choice of zero. The key is to pick zeros that have a high level of asset cover and a negative hurdle rate – that is the amount by which the value of the assets can fall each year and still leave enough to pay holders (see below).

For a direct investment, financial advisers recommend a minimum investment of £10,000. They can be bought through stockbrokers or financial advisers. For those with less cash to spare or who simply want to spread the risk, a fund of zeros might be a better option.

Jargon buster

The zero market is full of jargon that is worth getting to grips with before taking the plunge.

Gross redemption yield (GRY): This is the annual compound growth rate that the zero is expected to provide. Investors who successfully use their Capital Gains Tax allowance to avoid tax on the investment can think of this as a net figure when comparing it to other investments. A GRY in the high double figures should probably be avoided.

Asset cover: This figure shows by how much the redemption price is covered. For example, if it is quoted at 120, then there are enough assets in the trust to cover the final price by 120 per cent (or 1.2 times).

Hurdle rate: This tells you by what percentage a Trust's assets must grow in value each year to meet its target. Zeros with a negative hurdle rate are more attractive because the assets would need to fall in value before failing to pay up. A hurdle rate of minus three per cent means the assets could fall by three per cent each year until the Trust is wound up and still have enough to pay zero holders.

Lump sums

If you come into a large lump sum that you want to use for school fees, you could think about paying it to the school in advance. These are called 'composition fees'. Most schools will offer a reasonable discount for fees paid in advance, particularly if the payment is for the whole period of your child's attendance. If a child's parents make the payments they do not attract inheritance tax. However, if someone else makes the lump sum payment, such as a grandparent, there could be inheritance tax implications.

If grandparents can afford to cover some or all of the fees on a regular basis from income instead of capital, then the payments may fall outside the inheritance tax bracket (see Chapter 13), however. Either way, grandparents should seek tax-planning advice before going ahead.

The Independent Schools Council Information Service has a useful leaflet on planning for school fees and has a guide to school bursaries and scholarships. Telephone 020 7798 1500 or visit *www.iscis.uk.net*.

11

Alternative investments

'The more alternatives, the more difficult the choice.'

Abbé D'Allainval, 1726

You and your children may get a big thrill from watching a bank balance, share price or investment fund grow over time, but many people want that little extra something from their investments. That is why many take an interest in 'alternative investments'. The name covers a broad spectrum ranging from collectibles, such as stamps, books and toys, to fine wine, paintings and furniture, with thousands of options in between.

High risk

Few investments are free of risk and alternative investments are no exception. In fact, financial advisers warn that they teeter at the top of the risk pyramid and that you should be prepared to invest for at least five years or more to have a chance of seeing a return.

Because of the risks, you should also only invest a small proportion of your total portfolio in alternatives.

Alternatives are not regulated by financial watchdogs like other financial investments, and it can be hard to get help if you are are sold a 'pup'. Your only option may be to report a supplier or dealer to trading standards officials or take them to court.

From reputable companies

It makes sense to buy any alternative investment, whether a bottle of vintage wine or an Edwardian chest of drawers, from a reputable company. Most will be members of a recognised trade body. For example, antique dealers may be members of the British Antique Dealers' Association or the Association of Art and Antique Dealers (see Chapter 12).

Apart from getting pleasure from owning such investments, investors hope that over time they will grow in value.

One big difference between an alternative investment and more conventional products is that the former is unlikely to produce an income. However the attraction of a nil income investment is that there is no income tax to pay.

Capital gains tax

Most alternative investments are potentially liable to Capital Gains Tax, though. An example might be an antique sideboard you bought 15 years ago and now sell for a profit (after expenses and taking into account any indexation or taper relief). As explained in earlier chapters, however, you can make use of your annual Capital Gains Tax allowance, £7,700 in the tax year 2002–2003, possibly to avoid a tax bill so as long as your investment has not skyrocketed in value.

Pros and cons

Paul Ilott, an adviser with Bates Investment Services, a national chain of Independent financial advisers, says alternative investments can be appealing but warns investors to bear in mind the hidden costs and dangers involved.

As Ilott says: 'Investing in valuables can prove profitable. British Rail Pension Fund invested in art in the 1970s and spent £40m on about 2,400 objects. By the end of the 1990s the Fund had achieved an overall similar return to that of UK equities.'

He adds: 'But there are no clearly regulated markets for valuables as there are for financial assets like equities and bonds.

'This means that you can never be sure of their true value and you certainly can't track their value in the same way as you might a portfolio of shares by scouring the financial press for share price details. There is also the downside that fashion tends to dictate what is valuable at any one point in time and that the pool of collectors for certain valuables can be very limited in size – making it difficult to sell when tastes change.'

Hidden costs

Investors need to take into account the costs of holding any sort of investment, as these will eat into the overall return.

With more common investments such as equities, on-going investment charges are often taken from the income produced by the investment, such as the dividends or interest. Ilott says: 'Alternative investments do not produce any income and investors therefore need to bear the ongoing costs for insuring their collection against loss or damage and for any special storage arrangements it might demand from their own resources.'

There are also initial costs to consider, such as the seller's commission and buyer's premium at art and antique auction houses. They usually amount to around 10–20 per cent plus VAT (selling is lower).

Investing in port

When a baby is born, parents, grandparents and godparents like to mark the occasion with a traditional gift. One popular option is to 'lay down' some port, which the child can either sell (hopefully at a profit) at the age of 18 or consume with family and friends at a coming of age birthday bash.

However according to Tuggy Meyer of the fine wine merchant Huntsworth Wine Company, based in Kensington, West London, 'Port is out of fashion at the moment and hasn't risen in value that much.' Nevertheless, he believes it makes a good gift for youngsters because of its ability to withstand the test of time.

He says: 'Port has higher alcohol content than wine so it keeps very well. If you lay it down at birth you needn't worry that it won't last.'

A typical vintage bottle costs around £20, though a top name port from 1994, deemed a good year, may be nearer £85.

Wine investments

Meyer says investing in wine has become a more popular alternative, with Bordeaux and Burgundy vintages attracting most attention.

A Bordeaux enthusiast, Meyer says it is key for wine investors to seek out a good wine merchant for advice: 'London is the fine wine investment capital of the world and there are at least 50 quality wine merchants in the city who have their own specialist knowledge. Very serious investors with a reasonable budget should buy from five or six different sources.'

Of the Bordeaux wines, he recommends 1982 and 1990, the latter offering better value for money.

A key consideration for an adult laying down wine for an infant is that the wine needs to be looked after carefully for 18 years or more. If it is stored at the wrong temperature then the investment could be lost. Meyer adds: 'Ideally wine should be stored in a dark, damp cellar at a constant temperature of 11 degrees centigrade. What's really important is that the temperature does not fluctuate.'

If looking after the wine at home is too much hassle, then investors can arrange for someone else to do it for them. One option is to store your wine at a bonded warehouse. Bonded wine does not attract duty or VAT, although there will be an annual management charge of around 0.5 per cent. Alternatively, wine merchants can store the wine on your behalf, most charging a few pounds a year for each case.

Insurance

Remember to think about insurance for your wine. A flooded cellar or burglary could wipe out your investment overnight.

My sister's father-in-law, who is French, learnt the hard way that insurance is an essential consideration. After he had built up a fine cellar of wine at his home in Paris, burglars broke in and stole the lot, leaving him out of wine and seriously out of pocket.

Prices

Wine can be bought and sold through merchants or through auctions. All the big auction houses, such as Bonham's, Sotheby's and Christie's, run regular wine auctions.

Wine prices can vary from merchant to merchant, so do your research in advance. *Decanter* Magazine and the Bordeaux Index, a wine merchant that publishes an index tracking the investment performance of wine, are just two useful London-based sources that also have websites (*www.decanter.com* and *www.bordeauxindex.com*). The internet is a great source for research on wine prices.

Beware of scams

Be careful not to get caught out by a get-rich-quick drinks investment scam. There are unscrupulous people out there who are only interested in parting investors and their cash. For advice on how to spot – and avoid – scams, take a look at the website *www.investdrinks.org*. If you have got sucked in, it also offers tips on where to go for help.

You may be able to protect yourself from losing money in such circumstances by making any purchase over £100 with a credit card. Under the terms of the Consumer Credit Act the credit card company may be liable to cover any loss.

Tax-free

One big attraction of wine investment is that individuals who buy it for their own use are not charged Capital Gains Tax if they later sell up at a profit. This is because the taxman categorises it as a wasting asset. But if you are regularly buying and selling large stocks of wine, the taxman might start to look at your position differently, so seek independent advice before becoming a wine wheeler-dealer.

Tangible asset

Wine is an unpredictable investment and if you choose the wrong wine or the wine values plummet there may be no gain at all. Meyer is philosophical about this. He says: 'In the end it doesn't really matter if the value of the wine fluctuates over the years. You still have a bottle of wine that is a tangible asset that you can enjoy. You can't say that about a share. If a company goes bust, all you have in the end is a worthless piece of paper.'

Champagne moment

Anyone tempted to lay down champagne on behalf of a newborn baby should probably think about cracking it open in celebration of a child's birth instead. Meyer says: 'Champagne is not such a good investment. It is quite expensive in the first place. There was a lot of hype around the millennium and many people got their fingers burnt.'

Antiques

Your children might be too young to appreciate the beauty of a piece of antique furniture or a painting. But at least mums and dads can use the item or take aesthetic pleasure from it until their offspring reach an age when they can make up their own minds about its value to them.

The antiques market has changed dramatically in the UK since the advent of the BBC's *Antiques Road Show* that has turned millions of households into antiques detectives. Tuggy Meyer is also an antiques dealer, and has seen a revolution in the market since the arrival of the programmes.

He says: 'The ground rules have been torn up as a result. Competition is intense and prices have shot up. That's great news for someone who already owned antiques but makes it much harder for someone wanting to get in for the first time.'

Antiques have never been a cheap form of investment but they have become more costly as owners of collectible pieces have become much harder bargainers.

Fashions change

Changing fashions can dramatically affect your chosen investment. There are no guarantees it will grow in value. As Meyer says: 'You could buy a painting for £10,000 now that might end up being worth £30,000 in five years' time or it might still be worth £10,000 which means it will have declined in value in real terms.'

Sought-after items can rise in price sharply over a short period, only to plummet as tastes change or a recession hits.

Furniture rises

According to the Antique Collectors' Club, the year 2000 was a strong year for antique furniture prices. The club's Antique Furniture Index, which measures prices from shops, fairs, markets and auctions across the UK, rose by 13 per cent. Particularly strong performers included oak and walnut furniture that rose by 17 per cent and 19 per cent respectively.

The club reckons antique furniture has outshone both the stock market and the housing market (excluding London) over the last three decades – although its figures do not take into account trading or selling margins.

Tough times

An economic recession can quickly change the dynamics of the collectibles market. Suddenly, people who are still interested in investing want to buy practical items such as a top quality chest of drawers. Meyer says: 'In tough times people look for higher quality and purity of design. They want something that is the best quality example of what they want. They don't want one that has been over-restored. It is sensible to do this even if it means paying a lot more to get it. The differential in price between the best quality item and the faulty item will increase sharply.'

Dealers

If using dealers to buy an antique, it is worth asking whether they will consider taking the item back at a future date and sell it for at least at the same price you paid. Most good dealers should agree to this and it can give buyers peace of mind.

Stamped out

Stamp collecting is a hobby often associated with children. It is a pastime that can educate and inform since many stamps commemorate historical events or depict images from around the world. However, stamp collections as an investment have fallen out of favour, and as a result the values have fallen. This is partly because the original collectors are dying off and younger generations are more interested in modern alternatives. Stamps were important for much of the twentieth century because they represented one of the main forms of communication. But now collectors are likely to get a greater buzz from picking up early examples of mobile phones or computer games.

First editions

Another popular pastime enjoyed by book-loving parents and grandparents is to seek out a first edition for their loved-ones, which could turn into a family heirloom or an investment goldmine. However if it is the first edition of a children's classic like a Beatrix Potter or Winnie the Pooh that you are after, then, rather than rummaging through the shelves of secondhand bookshops or visiting charity shops, these days – according to collecting expert Lorne Spicer, who has her own slot on television's *This Morning* and a weekly column in the *Mail on Sunday* – you are more likely to have to fork out a fortune at auction. As she says: 'Charity shops now get their books valued, so you are unlikely to stumble upon a first edition there.'

She adds: 'One of Beatrix Potter's first edition Peter Rabbit books recently sold at auction for £18,000. What is particularly interesting about that was she had it printed herself because no publisher would consider it.'

Modern classics

Parents who picked up a signed first edition of JK Rowling's first book, *Harry Potter and the Philosopher's Stone*, could be on to a good investment. According to Spicer, it could now reach between £12,000 and £15,000 at auction. 'The later books are not likely to attract the same prices,' she adds.

Spicer has a useful tip for buyers of new books signed by the author: 'In a couple of generations' time it may be difficult for the owner to prove that the signature is genuine. You should try and take a photo at the signing and keep it with the book. The same goes for soccer fans who collect football programmes with players' signatures.'

Film of the book

Many investors like to collect memorabilia from films such as branded mugs or china models of the characters.

Spicer reckons one area to consider is the limited edition pottery figures based on characters from Harry Potter, such as those issued by Royal Doulton. She says: 'In the 1960s there was a range of Beatrix Potter figures. But a black dog called the Duchess with Flowers proved unpopular because of its colour and didn't sell. The manufacturer withdrew it from the range, which immediately made it a collectable. In the collecting market it is now worth around £1,000 when the other characters are worth just £50.'

Another example of how the odd one out can offer attractive returns occurred with the range of figurines based on the mice characters from the Brambly Heath books by Jill Barklem. As Spicer says: 'The character Mr Toadflax was initially produced with a very long tail between his legs. This was withdrawn because it was considered it looked rude and was replaced. The new version would now attract between £30–£40 whereas the "rude Mr Toadflax" would attract nearer £800.' She adds: 'This could well happen with the Harry Potter range if one of the characters does not sell or has to be changed in some way.'

Teddy bears

You can't get much more traditional than a teddy bear as a first gift for a newborn. And they can make a good investment if you buy the right one. One of the most famous manufacturers is Stieff. It produced a limited edition Titanic Bear in 1997 for £120. According to Spicer, that would now fetch around £350 at auction.

For those with an eye on a modern alternative, there are beanbag toys to consider. Beanie Babies, produced by US company Ty Warner, have been manufactured in their millions over the last few years and were responsible for sparking a massive collection craze for the toys in households across the world. But as Spicer says: 'If you want to invest in these you really have to know your stuff and know which ones are the most collectable.'

Walt Disney produces similar bean-filled toys based on popular characters such as Winnie the Pooh. Spicer says: 'These are probably a better investment because you are covering three potential collecting markets: collectors of Winnie the Pooh memorabilia, collectors of Disney memorabilia and Beanie Baby collectors. With a Ty Beanie Baby, you have only got the Beanie Baby collectors.'

Toy cars

Grandparents on the look out for a Christmas or birthday present that will please on the day as well as bring potential financial pleasure in the future could also think about toy cars. Not just any toy cars though. The ones that gain in value are the traditional die-cast Corgi cars where each vehicle is made from metal poured into a mould. They do not cost much more than about £10 or £15 new, but can soon become collectable.

Spicer again: 'Film-related cars always do well. They've recently brought out a car based on the one that featured in the film *Back to the Future*. And James Bond cars are also a good bet.'

12 Property

'Property has its duties as well as its rights.'

Thomas Drummond, 1838

Inflation may have been tamed in recent years, but try telling that to homebuyers attempting to get a foot on the first rung of the property ladder. And what will it be like for our children's generation? I live in a residential area of South West London, where house prices have almost trebled since I moved in with my family in 1994. There is some feel-good factor to be gained from seeing such increases in value, but unless my family and I were intending to move out of London, we will not be cashing in on these investment gains.

At a school coffee morning recently, other parents were also lamenting the price rises. Most reckoned that they could not afford to move somewhere bigger in the same area. Worse still, they calculated that they could no longer afford to buy their own houses had they been moving into the area.

First-time buyers

There has been much publicity lately about how tough it has become for essential workers, including teachers and nurses, to find affordable properties in London. Mortgage rates are at an historic low, but house prices are not. In mid 2001 the average value of a first-time buyer property in London was over £133,000. It is not hard to see why first-time buyers are struggling.

Typically, lenders will only advance loans of three times salary. Even assuming a 10 per cent deposit, a first-timer would still need to be earning a salary of £40,000 a year in order to get a big enough mortgage.

Even outside London house prices are beyond the reach of many of those attempting to make their first foray into house purchase.

Next generation

No one knows what will happen to house prices in future. But what we do know is that in the last three decades they have gone from strength to strength with increases averaging around seven per cent a year, with one or two downturns and recoveries along the way.

If the trend for house prices to outpace earnings continues, then how will the next generation get their feet on the ladder? Many parents, and I include myself among them, worry how their children will be able to afford their first home 10 or 20 years from now.

Buy-to-let

One option worth considering is to buy a property for your offspring now and let it out until they are old enough to make use of it themselves. The buy-to-let property market has been booming in the last few years, partly because the demand in the letting market has been strong.

But mortgage lenders have also started offering much more attractive mortgage deals to would-be landlords. Lenders scrutinising a buy-to-let purchaser take into account the potential rental income from the property rather than looking at the borrower's earnings.

The low mortgage rates of recent years have also made the risks involved seem less daunting and rising house values in many areas have provided an extra boost.

Planning ahead

Savills Private Finance, a London-based independent financial adviser, specialises in this field and has noticed a rise in demand from parents planning ahead for their children.

Simon Jones, associate director, says: 'We think buying a property is a good way of diversifying a portfolio. A good time to do it is when you reach your 40s or 50s when you have hopefully started to build up some wealth. Property has been a sound investment historically. Rental income tends to rise in line with inflation rather than house prices so demand should be there. It should also make a sound growth investment depending on where you buy.'

He adds: 'Parents can invest for themselves initially and decide later whether or when to pass the property to their children.'

Raising cash

Savills says there are several methods of raising money to buy a home for your kids. Most buy-to-let loans allow a maximum 75 per cent loan, although some will offer 95 per cent if your children are older and going to live in it.

If you do not have enough spare money for a deposit, you can look at the amount of equity you have in your main home and raise the money by re-mortgaging. Some parents re-mortgage for the full amount of the new property purchase.

Affordability

However, Savills warns that the key to successful buy-to-let investing is affordability and stresses it is important to know how much you can afford in monthly interest payments. A fixed rate mortgage deal over a number of years can help you budget more easily.

Savills advises buy-to-let investors to charge rents high enough to cover both the mortgage repayments and any management and maintenance costs. If you use a managing agent to look after the property, that will reduce your rental income but cut down on the hassle involved.

Hedge against inflation

If you are worried your children will not be able to afford to buy a property when they reach adulthood you can think about buying the property now and then transferring it into their name when they are 18. You will probably need to act as a guarantor on the loan even at that point until they are earning enough to be able to take on the mortgage themselves.

Bare trusts

It is possible to hold the property in the child's name from an earlier age if it is held in a bare trust but you will have to seek the advice of a legal or tax expert on how to set that up.

If you hold the property in your own name and change ownership later, you need to watch for the tax implications. In the eyes of the taxman you would effectively be selling the property and so trigger a capital gain, and potentially Capital Gains Tax.

Savills recommends that parents who are buying as a hedge against inflation should choose an area where prices are likely to rise steadily, such as London or the South East. The rental yield will be lower, however.

University digs

When your children go off to university they need somewhere to live, but often all they find is mediocre accommodation at a high rental. One way to make sure your kids have a decent place to live is to buy a property in the town they are studying. And if you organise it properly they will also save on rent and earn a little extra on top.

You can think about buying the property yourself with a view to making money out of the investment while they are at university, both from the rental raised from letting rooms to other students and through a capital gain. However, three of four years of a student course may not be long enough to make much, if any, capital gain. Remember that there are big costs involved in buying and selling a property. When buying you face legal bills and stamp duty charges (if the property costs over

£60,000). And then there is the cost of furnishing the home to a reasonable standard. When a property is let out there are strict rules on what furnishings can be used. Finally, when you sell up, there will be estate agency fees and more legal costs.

Over 18

If your child is over 18, you can also think about buying the property in your child's name with you providing the deposit and acting as guarantor for the mortgage. This arrangement offers some tax advantages because it is your child's main residence. Mike Warburton, tax partner at national accountancy firm Grant Thornton, believes the university buy-to-let strategy is such a good idea that he has done it himself, for both his son and his daughter. He says: 'They both took out mortgages in their own names and I provided the guarantees. They rented out their rooms to fellow students and didn't have to pay any rent themselves.

'The mortgage and maintenance costs can be offset against the rental income for income tax purposes. My daughter rented out her house to five others. She was able to offset five-sixths of the costs. Since she was the sixth person living there but not paying rent she could not offset the full amount.'

For more information on the taxation of rental income ask your tax office for the leaflet IR150.

Another tax-efficient option is to make use of the rent-a-room allowance. This allows homeowners to earn rent from a room in their house of up to £4,250 a year without paying income tax. However if you use this option, you cannot also claim for expenses.

Property funds

You could also consider a property Unit Trust, Open Ended Investment Company or Investment Trust that invests in property. But take care when selecting a fund as portfolios vary dramatically. There are funds that invest only in property shares and some that invest purely in commercial property.

13

Passing on your wealth

'You can't take it with you.'

Proverb

Most people prefer not to think about death. Nor do they normally enjoy thinking about tax. But the harsh fact is that death and taxes are inextricably linked. For when we die, the long arm of the taxman reaches beyond the grave in a bid to grab a large chunk of our hard-earned savings and investments. The annual inheritance tax bill adds up to around £2.2 billion, much of it paid unnecessarily through lack of financial planning.

Some people might wonder why they should worry what happens to their money and belongings if they are dead. But others, plan ahead so that their children and grandchildren, rather than the Inland Revenue, enjoy their lifetime's savings.

Tax bill

You do not have to be seriously rich to think about inheritance tax issues.

Rising house prices, especially in London and the South East, are pushing more estates into the inheritance tax bracket. And it is not just house prices you have to think about.

If you own your own home, have built up some savings, a few privatisation shares, a handful of bonds and one or two items like paintings or valuable antiques, you can easily end up leaving quite a substantial estate.

Not all our worldly goods are hit for inheritance tax. Each person has an inheritance tax exemption that usually rises by the rate of inflation each tax year. In the tax year 2002–2003, the amount that can be left to relatives without attracting inheritance tax is £250,000. Anything over that amount attracts inheritance tax at a flat rate of 40 per cent. At the time of writing, the government was rumoured to be planning changes that would allow more middle-income families to escape the tax.

Wealth warning

The only way of knowing whether your estate could be heading for an inheritance tax bill is to monitor the value of all your assets and possessions regularly. You may not fall into the inheritance tax bracket at the moment, but a few years down the line, the value of your house and your shares may have risen sharply enough to take your estate over the edge.

When doing your sums, do not forget to add in any debts. They are deducted from your estate on death.

The decision on whether you should reduce the potential tax burden by passing on your wealth before you die must depend on your own financial circumstances and your feelings for your offspring. However, it is essential not to become too obsessed about passing the money down the generations at the expense of landing yourself in a financial mess in your old age.

Financial gifts

If you have calculated that you will have plenty of money to live on and are certain you want to pass on some of it to the next generation, then there are several options available.

The taxman offers a range of exemptions that allow gifts to be made tax-free, or at least potentially tax-free.

Married partners

Gifts made between married partners are tax-free, as are gifts to charities and mainstream political parties. So when someone dies, the gifts are not included in the deceased person's estate when calculating a potential tax bill.

Lifetime gifts

Parents or grandparents can pass down cash gifts of any size during their lifetime to the next generation – or to anyone else for that matter. These are called 'lifetime gifts' or 'potentially exempt transfers'. If the donor lives for seven years after making the gift, then there is no inheritance tax to pay. Nor is there tax to pay if the size of the estate, including the value of the gifts, adds up to no more than the annual exemption.

The grandfather of a friend has taken action recently to reduce the chances of an inheritance tax bill. He gave all his grandchildren money to put in children's savings accounts. And because it is he who has made the gifts, there will be no need for their parents to worry about any income affecting their tax positions.

As explained in earlier chapters, any income earned on gifts made by parents risk being taxed as part of the parents' income, if the annual income exceeds £100 for each parent.

Gifts with reservation

There are exceptions to the lifetime gifts rule, such as giving a home to your grandchildren yet continuing living in the house rent-free. This is called a 'gift with reservation'. In these situations, there is a chance the value of the home may still end up being added into your estate, so always seek the professional advice of an accountant or solicitor before you set up such an arrangement.

Non-cash gifts

Another pitfall to watch out for when passing on non-cash gifts is Capital Gains Tax. You may pass on the gift to your relative for nothing, but the Inland Revenue treats the transaction as if the donor had received the full market value.

You then may face a Capital Gains Tax charge on the gift if the value has risen significantly since you bought it. You can of course take into account any indexation or taper relief and your annual Capital Gains Tax allowance when making the decision, but it is best to get professional guidance first.

Another option is to transfer the assets into a discretionary trust. The rules mean you can defer paying the capital gains until the trustees sell the asset (more details later). The gift can still attract inheritance tax under the seven-year rule.

Tapered tax

Even if you do not quite make the full seven years, the tax bill for the person who received your gift may not be that big.

The tax on lifetime gifts is tapered: if you die within the first three years, the whole gift attracts inheritance tax but it reduces to 80 per cent between the third and fourth years, 60 per cent between the fourth and fifth, 40 per cent between the fifth and sixth and 20 per cent between the sixth and seventh.

Totally tax-free

There are other gifts that you can make without fear of the money attracting inheritance tax. Under the 'small gifts exemption' you can give up to £250 a year to as many people as you like. But if you exceed the £250 limit, even by £1, the gift will no longer be covered by the small gifts exemption. Instead, it would fall into the so-called 'annual exemption', a separate tax break that lets you give away £3,000 in a tax year.

Anyone can give away up to £3,000 in one tax year in this way. You can carry the allowance, or the balance of the amount if you have given away less than £3,000, forward for one year but after the second year the chance is lost.

Gifts from income

The taxman also lets you make regular gifts out of income without attracting inheritance tax when you die. These might be annual gifts for birthdays or Christmas or even school fees for grandchildren.

Mike Warburton, tax partner at accountants Grant Thornton in Cheltenham, Gloucestershire, says: 'This is a much neglected aspect of inheritance tax planning and can work well for those who have income well in excess of their expenditure. So long as you do not affect your standard of living by making these gifts, then the taxman will exclude them from your estate. It is wise to write a letter to the taxman when the arrangement is set up so there is no argument later on. You also need to take care where the money comes from. You are not allowed to dip into your capital to make these payments nor must you use capital to subsidise any income you may be giving up by making the gifts.'

Wedding bells

The taxman likes a wedding. So much so that he generously allows each parent to give up to £5,000 to each of their children, including stepchildren and adopted children, free of inheritance tax. Grandparents and other relatives may give £2,500 and others outside the family may give £1,000. The gifts must be made before the wedding takes place.

The Inland Revenue has some useful leaflets on inheritance tax, including how it is calculated and how much you can give away each year without the risk of a tax bill. Contact the Inland Revenue for copies and more information about inheritance tax on 0115 974 2400 if you live in England or Wales or visit the website at *www.inlandrevenue.gov.uk*

Trust funds

You don't have to live in 'It Girl' circles to include trust funds as part of your inheritance tax planning. Parents or grandparents are often keen to pass their wealth on and yet still maintain some control over the money until the youngsters are old enough to manage it. You can arrange for a lawyer or accountant or financial adviser with trust experience to set up a suitable trust so that your money falls outside your estate and yet allows you to have some say in who has access it and when.

Growth investments

To avoid facing any potential income tax and Capital Gains Tax bills from the underlying investment in a trust, you generally must not receive any of the benefits from the investments yourself. It may be better to choose investments that are unlikely to produce income or any capital gains in excess of your annual tax exemption.

Warburton says that typical investments that can be considered in this category include zero dividend preference shares. Zeros do not attract income tax and if annual Capital Gains Tax exemptions are used wisely then CGT may also be avoided (see Chapter 11 for more information on zeros).

There are many different types of trusts to meet different needs so you should always seek legal and financial advice before making a final decision. Bear in mind that there will be costs involved in both the setting up and running of the trust. The main ones you are likely to come across are accumulation and maintenance trusts and discretionary trusts.

Accumulation and maintenance trusts

These are normally most suitable for people who have a large estate and are most concerned about inheritance tax. You do have to pay capital gains on the investments as soon as you put them into the trust, but so long as you live for at least seven years after setting up the trust there will be no inheritance tax charged to the estate.

These trusts may fit the bill if you want your children or grandchildren to receive a gift but do not want them to have the right to the income and capital straight away; entitlement to the income normally occurs when they turn 25.

In the meantime the income must be 'accumulated' in the trust, although you can arrange for it to be used for a child's benefit at any time, such as for school or university fees or if it is needed to pay for care due to ill health.

You can also make arrangements for any children born after the trust is set up, so long as you say from the outset that this might happen. However, once one beneficiary starts receiving any income from the trust, no new names may be added.

You may also be able to keep the capital out of reach of the children for longer than the income if you are worried that access to large sums of money will lead them off the straight and narrow.

Discretionary trusts

Discretionary trusts are mostly used by people who want to give away assets but are concerned that the recipients might squander them. So parents who are worried that a daughter might make a bad marriage or a son might spend the whole lot on drugs can consider a trust to keep some control over the assets.

They are not normally chosen for their tax advantages, although they do allow you to defer and potentially reduce Capital Gains Tax, the initial transfer of assets into a discretionary trust attracting no such tax. However, if the trust or the beneficiary then sells the assets a tax charge will be triggered.

The base cost of the assets is set at the date you bought them and not at the date they were transferred into the trust.

Discretionary trusts are more flexible than accumulation and maintenance trusts because the decisions on how the income and capital is distributed can be made by the trustees when changing circumstances demand. If you want more control of the assets yourself, you can become one of the trustees. This can be particularly useful if you have several beneficiaries of the trust but want to delay the decision about who gets what.

While a discretionary trust may make it easier to pass assets to younger generations, it is not particularly tax efficient when it comes to inheritance tax. You will face a 20 per cent bill on assets over £250,000 (in the tax year 2002–2003) when you transfer the assets into the trust, and as much as 20 per cent more may be charged if you fail to survive seven years.

Draw up a will

Probably the most important first step in planning how to pass on your wealth to the next generation is to draw up a will. Two-thirds of us do not have one and those of us who do often stick it in a drawer and forget about it when we should be updating it from time to time.

If you die without a will, there are strict intestacy rules that decide what happens to your estate. This can cause extra pain for grieving families trying to sort out any confusion. In England and Wales, if you are married, only the first £125,000 of your estate plus your personal possessions will automatically go to your surviving partner. Your widow or widower will be allowed an income from half of the remainder. The other half goes to your children. Many houses are worth well over £125,000 these days, and without a will you risk your property having to be sold to meet the demands of the intestacy laws. The laws are slightly different in Scotland but the message is the same: make a will and avoid unnecessary pain.

Superstition

Many people put off organising a will because they feel superstitious about discussing their own deaths. That's how I used to feel. But once you have children you start to worry about what might happen to their financial security if the worst happens. My husband and I finally got round to drawing up wills after our eldest was born. That was nine years ago and until recently I did not know where they were stored in the house, although I had a vague recollection that our solicitor had kept copies.

I became less complacent recently, when we started planning for a trip to a friend's wedding in Latin America. Our children decided they did not want to come with us because of the number of injections required before travelling. The result was that we decided to leave them behind in the loving and capable hands of my mother and my husband's father and his wife.

Appropriate arrangements

But then I started to worry about what might happen if we never made it back. I wondered if our wills contained the appropriate arrangements, financial and practical, for our children's future. We did not have time to update our wills before travelling, so it was with some trepidation that we set off on the trip. Fortunately, it all went without a hitch but it has sparked us into action and we are now in the process of renewing the legal paperwork.

Life insurance

Life insurance is a crucial foundation in the financial plans of any parent with young children. Both my husband and I have made sure we are well insured. My own father died when I was a young teenager and if it had not been for his life insurance policy my mother would have faced financial meltdown on top of the emotional distress.

Most people want to provide for their families should the worst happen and to do so need not be that expensive. Term assurance is the cheapest type of life insurance and you take out a plan that lasts for a set period. People often take out a plan to cover the years when their financial commitments are at their peak, such as when the children are young, perhaps at private school, and there are mortgage payments to meet.

An alternative is a whole of life plan, which is more expensive but which covers you until death, whenever that may be. You may also take out an endowment plan that combines life assurance with savings.

Life insurance plans are also useful for inheritance tax planning. They can be written in trust so that when you die, the proceeds of the policy will fall outside your estate and the money can be used to cover any tax owed.

The Association of British Insurers has a guide to the different types of life insurance available. Visit its website at *www.abi.org.uk*.

14

Lessons in money

'Annual income twenty pounds, annual expenditure nineteen nineteen six, result happiness. Annual income twenty pounds, annual expenditure twenty pounds ought and six, result misery.'

David Copperfield, by Charles Dickens

Schoolchildren may think that lessons in personal finance are about as gripping as double Latin. But in an increasingly complex financial world, it is a subject worth learning fluently by the time they grow up. Even if they learn about money and how to manage it at home, they probably need help consolidating that knowledge in the classroom. The government is so concerned that children are leaving school ignorant of some of the most basic money matters, that it has been compelled to add personal finance to the curriculum. And so, since September 2000, the subject has been taught to youngsters in the UK incorporated within other lessons ranging from maths and information technology to religious education and history.

As each academic year passes, personal finance takes on an even greater role in children's formal education. By September

2002, the subject must be included formally as part of the 'consumer rights and responsibilities' module of citizenship studies.

Helping to underline the message that money is an important fact of life from birth to retirement are a wide range of initiatives drawn up by different organisations such as the Personal Finance and Education Group (PFEG) and the Financial Services Authority. Banks and building societies and other financial institutions also work hard to help teach children about money by devising study packs, websites, competitions, games and school visits.

Mini bank branches

Some high street banks even allow children to set up mini bank branches in schools where pupils can take on the role of a supervisor, take deposits from other children or put in and withdraw small amounts of their own money.

PFEG, a charitable organisation funded by financial groups including the Association of Investment Trust Companies, the Association of Unit Trusts and Investment Funds and the British Bankers' Association, is spearheading a campaign that aims to help 400 secondary schools across England prepare for the compulsory inclusion of personal finance in the curriculum. It provides training for teachers and a wide range of teaching materials. To back this up it also operates a website that offers guidance on how to include the topic of personal finance within a range of existing curriculum subjects. There are also case studies of schools that have already made progress in teaching about money matters.

Wendy van den Hende, chief executive of PFEG, says: 'Too often children leave school without knowing how to open a bank account or write a cheque.'

Not all children have the same gaps in their knowledge. Research has shown that those from poorer backgrounds have a much greater understanding about cash and how to budget. Youngsters from better-off families are more likely to be ignorant about cash but have more knowledge about credit cards and even the stock market.

PFEG is keen to get over the message that all young people

must be taught more about finance and that they require a better grounding than their parents ever needed. For example, borrowing money is now a fact of life for most of those who opt to go on to university after school. With financial help from the state shrinking rapidly, students need to be first-class students in managing debt.

Sales pressure

School leavers and graduates also need to be well prepared for the inevitable onslaught they will face from financial services providers from almost the first day they start work. They will face intense pressure from sales people, adverts and junk mail to take out some product or other, whether it is a pension, a cheap loan, a mortgage or insurance. They need to know how to separate the wheat from the chaff.

The Financial Services Authority (FSA) is taking the issue seriously. The watchdog has a whole department devoted to devising strategies to help all consumers, including schoolchildren, tiptoe through the minefield of products and issues. In October 2001, after researching secondary schoolchildren's weak points in money matters, the FSA launched its Colossal Cards initiative. The scheme centres around a series of giant cardboard cards and related support material to help teachers of 11 to 16 year olds teach youngsters about credit and debit cards. This scheme was devised following a successful programme for primary schools called Mega Money that featured giant coins.

Such materials can help teachers get to grips with passing on the message clearly to children.

Mini enterprise

PFEG has already inspired many schools in the UK to weave personal finance imaginatively into the existing curriculum. I covered one of these programmes for a piece I wrote for *Financial Mail on Sunday* which showed how a group of 13 to 14 year olds at Broadwater School in Godalming, Surrey, set up their own mini enterprise to make Christmas cards.

The scheme was a success with the pupils learning not only

about card design techniques but also about financial essentials such as buying equipment and cheque writing and understanding payslips. The project covered its costs enough to make a £10 payment to each student, some of whom used the money to set up their first bank account.

Other financial organisations offer useful background material for eager students of personal finance. They include ProShare, which promotes wider share ownership and organises an annual investment contest for schools as well as providing teaching materials. It has a useful website at *www.proshare.co.uk*.

NatWest bank has run a Face2Face with Finance programme in schools for many years.

Start young

Brian Capon at the BBA believes that teaching children about money should not remain purely within the classroom walls. He says: 'Children can learn loads about dealing with and managing money simply by accompanying their parents shopping. By letting them spend their pocket money in a shop they can see how the process works. They will soon learn how much things cost. There are educational games they can play too, such as the obvious ones of shop, where one child can be the shopkeeper and another the shopper. It can help them get used to numbers and hone their counting skills.'

Days out

One Christmas a few years ago, I suggested a feature for *Financial Mail on Sunday* on the subject of museums and money. I wanted to find out which museums focused on money or related issues. Some people thought me eccentric and asked if I really thought my children would enjoy spending the run up to Christmas learning about money in fusty old museums when they could visit Hamley's toy shop instead? But I argued that Christmas is the perfect time to teach children about money and how it came about, when such large sums are lavished on so many of them.

I went ahead with the research and, with the help of my daughters, investigated the options. At the time there was a temporary exhibition on the history of income tax at the Inland Revenue headquarters in Somerset House, London. To my surprise it was extremely educational, well presented and interesting. Amongst many other things, I learnt that the income tax was just 10p in the pound when it was first introduced two centuries ago and that it was raised from property owners to help fund a war with France.

We also visited the British Museum where there was an exhibition devoted to monetary union through the ages. It was interesting seeing European Monetary Union put in an historical context. I admit this was a bit highbrow for my kids, but I enjoyed it. There was plenty for them to look at too, including coins from different eras. A photograph of a glass case of glittering gold Roman coins still adorns our wall at home.

That was a fascinating visit. But in our view, the most illuminating of all was to the Bank of England museum. It is a real treasure trove of information about how money makes our world go round and is located behind the Bank of England building in Lombard Street in the City of London. It was not all about education. I was also able to purchase a few essential Christmas gifts including a chocolate gold bar for my nephew and a bottle of Bank of England port for my brother-in-law.

I can think of no better way to start learning about money.

ACKNOWLEDGEMENTS

I would like to thank everyone who has helped me by supplying information and ideas for the book.

Particular thanks go to all the friends, family and contacts who shared with me their experiences and stories. A big thanks to my sister Laura and brother John for helping me to recall events and anecdotes from our own childhoods.

Thanks also to all the financial experts I have quoted throughout the text, in particular Mike Warburton of accountancy firm Grant Thornton, who guided me expertly through the minefield of inheritance tax. Also to Witan and Quill Communications for their support and encouragement.

Last but not least, a big thank you to Jeff Prestridge, personal finance editor of *Financial Mail on Sunday* with whom I have worked for more than five years. His professionalism and love of the subject of personal finance have been an inspiration to me.

BIBLIOGRAPHY

Here are some books that helped enlighten me in the course of my research:

Which? Way to Save and Invest, published by Which? Books

Be your own Financial Adviser, by Jonquil Lowe, published by Which? Books

Financial Mail on Sunday Complete Guide to Personal Finance, by Jeff Prestridge, published by Random House

Positive Parenting, by Elizabeth Hartley-Brewer, published by Vermilion

Oxford Dictionary of Quotations, 6th edition

The New Penguin Dictionary of Modern Quotations, Penguin

Index

Jump

At the time of launching *Jump*, the savings plan for children, numerous savings plans and investment products were being marketed at parents for children. There were bank accounts, with their children's clubs and magazines, in abundance – designed for short-term easy-access savings – but very few plans designed for children and investing for the longer-term.

The Witan Investment Trust is a Global Growth investment trust, (one of the three largest trusts in the UK) and through investing in the world's biggest companies, has delivered consistently strong, long-term investment returns to its shareholders, since 1909.

Many of our shareholders are parents and grandparents, so when we asked them why they had originally invested in Witan, we were not entirely surprised to find that they saw Witan, with its internationally diversified investment strategy as an ideal vehicle to save for their children's and their grandchildren's university education, their first car, a deposit on their first home and so forth.

The Trust aims to deliver consistent, long-term performance without excessive risk, making it a good investment choice when investing for children, and the ideal platform for the *Jump* savings plan.

Think of *Jump* as a 'wrapper'. In the same way that you may have chosen an Investment Trust, Unit Trust or OEIC and invested up to £7,000 in that fund through an ISA, invest in *Jump* and you will be investing in Witan.

The *Jump* savings plan has been designed to offer you maximum flexibility. Your account is designated with the initials of the child. You can invest a lump sum in *Jump*, and you can top it up whenever you like. You can also invest through regular savings, from as little as £25 per month (or quarter) or lump sum from £100. You can stop and re-start your savings as you like, and you can cash in at any time, without penalty.

Our charges are low too, compared with similar stock-market based investment plans. We don't apply an initial charge and share dealing is 1% (subject to a minimum of £1.25 per deal), plus 0.5% Government Stamp Duty for share purchases (payable on all shares bought and sold).

Thousands are investing with *Jump* for a better start in life. Can we do the same for someone special in your life?

If you would like more information on *Jump*, call 0800 082 81 80 or visit us at *www.jumpsavings.com*